Valley of the Skookum

Four Years of Encounters with Bigfoot

Sali Sheppard-Wolford

Foreword by Autumn Williams

Pine Winds Press

Pine Winds Press
An imprint of Idyll Arbor, Inc.

Cover Art: Scott Davis
Cover Design: Pat Kenny
Interior Pictures: Sali Sheppard-Wolford and Autumn Williams
Pine Winds Press Editor: Thomas M. Blaschko

ISBN 0-937663-11-5
ISBN-13 9780-937663-11-0

For Youtle Tum Tum and Emily,

and for my daughter with the sunbeams in her hair

Foreword

I was born on October 20, 1973... six years to the day after Roger Patterson and Bob Gimlin filmed the famous Bluff Creek Bigfoot footage. Some would call that a remarkable coincidence, given the fact that my family subsequently encountered these large hairy bipeds over a period of several years in the late 1970s. In 2003, also perhaps coincidentally, I had the opportunity to interview Bob Gimlin on television and to return to Bluff Creek with him for the first time since that October day in 1967.

For the last 15 years, I have studied the Sasquatch phenomenon. My childhood experiences and those of my family have shaped my life to a degree that I can't begin to know.

Early on, I noted that there were two types of witnesses to this phenomenon: incidental and long-term. Incidental witnesses may get a clear but brief look at a Sasquatch crossing the road in front of their car. No matter how much they are questioned, they can only give limited information about their sighting (e.g., the color of the creature, its gait, stride, etc.). All things equal, I decided that my time would be better spent interviewing long-term witnesses: those who, like my family, claimed ongoing encounters near their residence.

I was taken aback by what I found. These people, from all across the country, claimed subtle details of interaction that were eerily similar to those my family experienced. But these details had never been published. The stories were too "out there" for most researchers to touch with a ten-foot pole (researchers are notoriously concerned about their own credibility). But I listened, holding judgment at bay. As the witnesses began to trust me, they would divulge further details, all more and more astounding... and increasingly familiar.

Throughout this research, however, I learned true skepticism. Not an all-encompassing disbelief (which seems to be the working definition of skepticism), but an ability to listen to a witness' story and separate fact from interpretation. Being skeptical and open-minded simultaneously is the key. Being open-minded does not make one a believer. It simply means that one allows for possibilities that present themselves to scrutiny.

There are a variety of socio-economic and cultural factors to consider when interviewing a long-term witness. Most are rural people who live on the outskirts of civilization. They often lack formal education. They very often lack technological equipment, even cameras. They are often "salt-of-the-earth" type people who are inquisitive and open-minded but are lacking in scientific sophistication. Add in whatever particular spiritual dogma they ascribe to and all of these factors tend to color how these events are perceived and related. Fantastic elements do not necessarily mean that Bigfoot-related events are not occurring. However, the *interpretation* is usually subjective, based upon their perception and belief system.

I asked my mother to tell me what happened in Orting from start to finish, to assuage the curiosity that has burned in me since I was a small girl. After begging her for years, she finally chose to write down the story in its entirety and I was thrilled. As it is with any witness, I am aware that her telling of the events is colored by her individual perceptions and understanding of the world around her. That which sounds fantastic to some is no surprise to others. Credibility, as with most things, is subjective.

I waited a long time to hear this story. I hope you enjoy it as much as I did.

Autumn Williams
February 2006

There are places on earth where mystery seems to live... where credible eyewitnesses claim to have seen creatures that science says do not exist. Most of these sightings are no more than a glimpse of something large and hairy on a darkened highway or a mountain trail. Then there are those of us who have lived with the mystery day after day and become a part of it.

Sali Sheppard-Wolford

Prologue

The wind paused to fill its cheeks, seeking direction for its next mighty onslaught. It blew fresh off the glaciers of Mt. Rainier, freezing everything in its path to a still-frame of winter glory.

Northwest natives knew the secret of the wind: With it came the low, mournful cries of Skookum, the great man-beast of the mountain. Generations of fathers and sons passed on the knowledge of the elusive tribe of giants. Skookums' grotesque likenesses graced Totem poles in each village and peopled campfire tales. Skookum was part of the Indian world.

Each year, at the first sign of autumn, Skookum would retire to the caves on the Great Mountain. They would stay there until the scent of the thaw reached their nostrils from the valley below.

Frozen days dragged on and the giants grew restless, longing to stretch their limbs. Finally, winter began to lose its hold on the land and mournful cries could be heard on the wind. The Natives rejoiced when they heard these cries; they knew it was not the wind, but the sounds of Skookum coming down from the mountain to walk the forest once again. Spring was not far behind.

Over the years, change came to the Carbon River valley. Native dwellings no longer dotted its banks. Natives went to live deeper in the forest. Loud men with pale faces took their place. These new men lived in box-like structures that never moved. To them, the cries of Skookum were just another icy gust, prompting them to add another log to the fire. The old ways mattered nothing to them. Skookum did not exist.

Skookum were aware of these pale creatures. They watched, hidden, when these new men killed for sport and cut tall trees to build their homes. These days, the wind carried the scent of blood, and fear filled the forest. In the old days the hairless ones had respected Skookum and each had lived in harmony with the other. Skookum felt confused; these new men respected nothing.

1977

As the warm breath of spring signaled the time for Skookum to walk the valley once again, the urge to do so was overwhelming. It was as much a part of them as the river that ran beside the trail. They would, as they always had, follow the clear waters of the Carbon River to the lower lands. But now, the trek would take Skookum close to the pale men's doors.

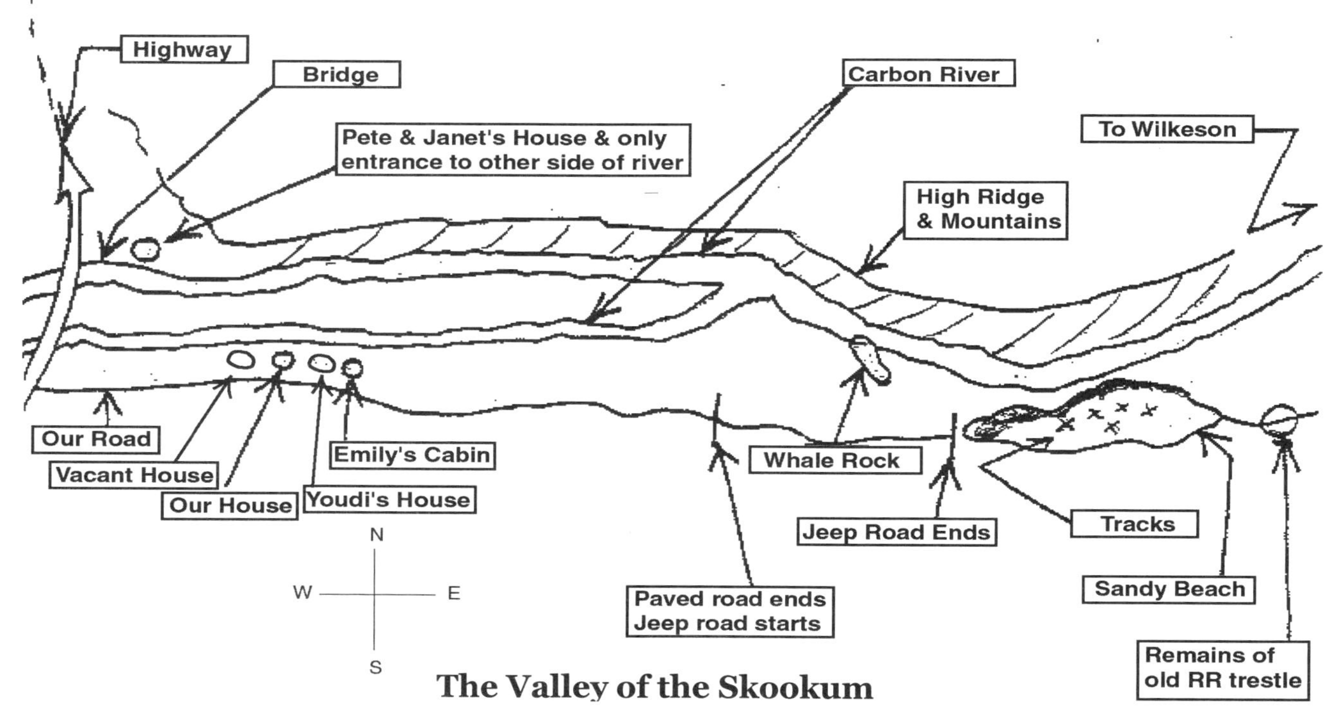

The Valley of the Skookum

Chapter One

And here were forests ancient as the hills
Enfolding sunny spots of greenery.

— Samuel Taylor Coleridge
"Kubla Khan"

Spring had come to the Northwest woods. Torrential rains left no corner dry. Though the deluge had ceased momentarily, a sodden canopy of maple and fir made it necessary to use the wipers as we threaded our way down an isolated road deep in the forests of Western Washington. Despite an occasional shaft of sunlight that managed to knife its way through the dense foliage, it still felt like dusk at 10:00 a.m.

I gazed through the foggy windshield at a primal world in which a pterodactyl could swoop down at any moment and carry off our tiny vehicle, passengers and all. There was no telling how long the forest had remained unchanged.

Limbs clutched at our car like gnarled hands, daring us to travel on. We were pressed on both sides by the thick green smell of decaying undergrowth.

I had heard people complain of the ceaseless rain in these forests, but I couldn't find fault when the result was such beauty. Sword ferns tall as a man bowed gracefully to let us pass as my husband, John, navigated the ever-narrowing road. At ground level, clumps of bleeding heart with lacy foliage and pink sprays of blossom lined the road. A carpet of lady slippers and yellow violets hid shyly beneath tall benefactors.

Rustic cabin on approx. 1 1/4 acre. River frontage, the ad read. Somewhere amongst all this beauty sat the small piece of land we were searching for. The sketchy directions given by the woman on the phone hadn't included an address. No houses had been visible for what seemed like several miles. I wondered if we were lost.

Then, to our left, the trees parted and a string of small cabins came into view. They seemed to sprout like mushrooms from the dank forest floor.

"This must be it," I said. "The one in the middle has a sign out front."

While my husband parked the car in the treacherous mud beside the road, I surveyed our surroundings. "Rustic" didn't begin to describe what I saw. "Rustic" is a kind word, bringing to mind braided rugs and flagstone fireplaces. This shack was dismal.

Its long, narrow shape was almost lost beneath a thick layer of moss. The walls were rotted clear through in places. A bent stovepipe protruded at a drunken angle from the green roof. Dingy, broken windows on either side of a gaping black doorway gave the appearance of a smiling wino. A set of rotting wooden stairs led into the mouth. Halfway down a mud-choked path, a crooked sign proclaimed, “HOUSE FOR SAL.” The “E” had long since worn away.

“Look at that, Sal!” John laughed. “The sign has your name on it.”

“Very funny.” I shot him a dirty look and stepped out of the car into ankle-deep mud. As I squished away from the car, my senses prickled. I had the distinct feeling we were being watched. Visions of a cranky hermit with a loaded shotgun flashed through my mind. I shivered and pulled my sweater close around me as I scanned the other two cabins, keeping close to my husband as I slid down the path behind him.

The other cabins looked empty. Their doors remained shut and limp curtains hung in the windows in the one to my left. I watched to see if the curtains moved. The windows were boarded over in the building to the right, but the door could burst open at any time. My eyes and ears told me we were alone, but some other sense told me otherwise. I tugged on John’s sleeve, and whispered.

“Do you get the feeling we’re not alone?”

He tugged his arm from my grasp. “God, Sal, don’t start that psychic crap. Your imagining things. There hasn’t been anybody around here since forever. Do you see tire tracks in the mud? Footprints on the path? Maybe you haven’t noticed that this rain makes it kinda obvious when someone’s been around.”

Silent like always, I followed John to the cabin. The rain was back and the path was becoming a creek.

John reached the rickety steps first and held out his hand to hoist me up. We stood in silence on the threshold, squinting into the silence of the cabin’s only room. To the left, a green enameled wood cook stove crouched like a cornered beast. Its oven door hung from one hinge. From the ceiling a single, bare light bulb hung. Above a rust-stained sink in a homemade stand, a long-necked faucet craned out from the wall. What drew me was a window above the sink, which hinted at the beauty beyond through the mildew on its gray-green panes.

The rest of the long, narrow room was empty. The whole cabin was no bigger than the kitchen of the house we now rented in town. Light shone through holes in the floor big enough to drop a cat through. The green, weathered interior was the back of the same thin boards that made up the green, weathered exterior. All that held this "rustic" cabin upright was a flimsy two-by-four framework. Loud, rhythmic plunking on the floor signaled where to find the holes in the roof. But at least it had electricity and running water.

John took a long, deep breath. "Well, it needs a little work, but what do you think?"

I snorted. "Is that anything like being a 'little pregnant'? It's a disaster. It's a shack. We'd be crazy to buy this place."

His face fell, pouting. "You're the one who's so gung-ho to live like pioneers. At least we can afford this place. We can always fix it up and add on."

He was right. I was the one who needed to find a place of our own outside of the city where we could raise our daughters. Sometimes dreams and reality don't quite match up. Dreams usually lose. "Okay," I said, "why don't we take a look at the rest of the property before we make any decisions?"

John shrugged. Back in the mud outside, we slipped and slid around the corner of the cabin, then made our way down another rickety flight of steps running down the hillside to the backyard. A faint path (still with no footprints, as John smugly pointed out) led us through a tangle of huckleberry bushes and vine maple. When we reached a sandy clearing, I stopped and glanced back. The small cabin was almost invisible in the vegetation but I could see that its deck hung out over this lower level, supported by questionable timbers. To our right sat a spider-infested outhouse with the iconic half-moon carved in the open door.

According to the owner's description, the lot was 80 ft wide and 360 ft long, give or take, depending on where the river flowed at any given time. There were no fences, but we could sort of guess at the boundaries.

We continued on. After the small clearing, the undergrowth became thick again. The path was sandy and much more pronounced. I had to wonder who, or what, used this well-worn path if no one was around. (Still no footprints, though.) The trail

Back of the house

ended abruptly at another high bank lined with huge rocks. John helped me over the rocks and we stood on a dirt road. A stretch of water-worn boulders led to a picturesque valley about a quarter of a mile across. On the far side loomed a densely forested ridge with the river at its base. I had never seen a more beautiful sight.

We looked at each other and scrambled like squirrels over the remaining rocks to the water.

Swollen with runoff from the rains, the river crashed and swirled through the pristine valley. There was no sign of civilization in any direction. In a deep pool beside us, the water was so clear that we could see huge fish swimming in lazy circles. We watched in awe as a salmon rose to pluck a spidery-looking water bug from the surface.

John was right; we could live here. Any doubts I'd had

The Carbon River at low flow, seen across the exposed rocks

disappeared with the splash of the fish's tail. The condition of the cabin was temporary... this scenery was forever. While John wandered off to the far end of the pool, I gazed into the distance upriver.

From the direction of the ridge, a blue-gray bird with an unbelievable wingspan and a long neck flew toward me. I wanted to shout to John but I was afraid I would frighten the bird away. Its flapping wings held me spellbound as it approached. It circled once, so close that I could see the black of its eye, then vanished while I watched. One second it was there, the next it was gone.

The back of my neck prickled as I scanned the sky. The bird was nowhere to be seen. I couldn't begin to explain where it had gone. I jumped when John spoke beside me.

"Can you imagine being the first person to ever see this place? They must have thought they'd found Heaven."

John bolted over the rocks in the direction of the cabins. "Race ya back," his voice came on the wind.

The mood shift caught me off guard. I was still looking for that damned disappearing bird and he was playing boy games. I took one last, unhelpful look at the empty sky and scrambled after him. By the time I reached the dirt road John was nowhere in sight. I stood still, calling his name several times, getting no response.

John was always playing childish games. He was probably behind some tree getting set to jump out at me. Then he'd run off, laughing with malicious glee. Looking at the silent woods, I just wondered where he was hiding. I took my time walking along the road, picking flowers as I went. I was in no mood to be frightened. It would serve him right to have to crouch behind some bush much longer than he had intended.

With each step I expected to hear the bushes rustle, followed by a loud shriek and John's hysterical laughter, but I was disappointed. I had walked deep into the woods before I noticed the absolute quiet.

No birds twittered. No twigs cracked. All the tiny noises of the forest that had accompanied our walk to the river were missing. The eerie silence engulfed me. I looked up and the sky was filled with ominous black clouds. Goosebumps not only popped up, they actually flowed over my flesh and I knew, I *really* knew, that I was being watched.

I told myself, "Don't panic. Don't panic. Don't..." Then a breeze blew by carrying a horrible stench like rotten eggs and garbage. I was not alone. I turned in the direction of the smell and a thump in my solar plexus confirmed that this was no game. "JOHN," I screamed and I bolted down the trail toward the cabins, dropping my flowers. (Not that I noticed at the time.)

The woods behind me erupted with a violent crashing. Stupid? Smart? I don't know, but I turned to face whatever it was. There was a large, dark brown something disappearing into the trees.

Somehow, this was worse than a charging monster. I ran mindlessly, tripping over my feet and landing with a hard thud in the damp sand. Hoisting myself up, I prepared to run, but noticed the forest suddenly felt normal again. The sun peeked through the clouds, birds chirped; the presence was gone. Whatever had been on the path with me had disappeared... just like that heron.

I felt like I was losing it. Were we buying property in the Twilight Zone?

For my own peace of mind, I had to know. I summoned up my last bit of courage and retraced my steps until I came upon the crushed flowers. Off to the side of the path, it looked like a tank had gone through the bushes. The brush was mangled to about ten feet in, then all destruction ended. Broken branches hung like dead snakes above my head. Whatever had torn this hole through the woods could have crushed me like a bug, but it had run in the opposite direction before disappearing. We had scared each other!

No footprints but my own were visible in the roughed-up sand of the path. That seemed odd, too, as if signs had been purposefully obscured. Then I remembered how large the brown shape had been. I forced myself to look up into the surrounding trees. Hanging from a limb above my head, a small clump of brown hair betrayed the visitor. I jumped, but couldn't reach it. With a long stick, I lifted some of it down. When I brought it to my nose, I caught a whiff of the sour odor I had smelled before.

It was then that the reality of the creature's size hit me. It had to be almost eight feet tall. But that was impossible. Bears didn't get that big, did they? *Of course bears didn't disappear either.* My knees threatened to fold as John's voice came faintly through the trees. "Sal? Saaaaaal? Where the hell are you?"

I stuffed the bit of hair into my sweater pocket and hurried up the path before I answered. I didn't want John to know what had happened. He wouldn't believe me and if he knew that something "funny" was occurring here, he would never agree to stay. Scared like hell, running from eight-foot-tall, hairy beasts...

Now I knew this was the place. There were mysteries here. Like the sign said, "HOUSE FOR SAL."

John came puffing up to where I stood. "Where have you been? I've been looking all over for you."

My anger flared. "Me? You're the one who ran off and left. I figured you were going to jump out and scare me, so I just took my own sweet time."

John rolled his eyes. "I wasn't trying to trick you. I ran to the car and you didn't show up. Then I went back to the river but you weren't there either. Now I can see why. You got lost. This is the wrong trail, you know. You sure you can handle leaving the city? Hey. what's that gross smell?"

"Uh, I think someone dumped some garbage around here. Let's go."

I was about to make some appropriate comeback to the crack about my wilderness skills, but then I saw an immense pile of rotting logs. I hadn't seen that on the way out, so I swallowed my retort, gazing around in wonder. On both sides of the path, huge logs were piled like the bones of a fallen giant. Alder and dogwood trees grew from their decaying carcasses and far above our heads their spindly limbs stretched toward the sparse warmth of the spring sun. The air was thick and dank as we walked through a world the wind would never reach. Sprouting from the knobby knees of fallen maples, lacy huckleberry bushes and maidenhair ferns clutched at our clothes with wispy fingers as we passed.

Even John was silenced by the beauty of this fairyland. We emerged behind the cabin with the boarded up windows. Okay, so I really had taken the wrong path back from the river. On the way to the car, I wondered why someone put boards on those windows when the glass still looked all right.

The rain had started again, big drops tapping lightly in the canopy of fir and maple. When we reached the car, I could tell John was ready to get back to town and buy the place. But there was one more place I wanted to see: a house for rent higher up on the mountain. I felt we should at least look at every possibility before we went home.

Back down that long, narrow road, just before we reached the highway, I noticed a row of overgrown brick caves set back in a field. I wondered what they could possibly have been for way out here.

On the drive up the mountain, I thought over my experience on the trail. I fingered the soft hair in my pocket as my mind wandered. Whatever creature I'd come upon had merely been curious; otherwise I wouldn't be here wondering what it had been. I would have been food instead.

And with that thought we reached our destination: Hucklechuck. The tiny settlement was a forty-five-minute drive from the cabin near Orting.

The rental wasn't hard to find; there were only about six buildings in the town proper. A handwritten sign in the window of the tiny, old schoolhouse read, "House for Rent. $50 Per Month." It was perched on a rise above the river. The door was open so we went in. The building's only room had windows on three sides. The top half of each was made of stained glass. On a sunny day the colors would play beautifully over the scarred hardwood floors inside. No holes in the floor, I noticed. Nice solid walls and a working roof. Not only that, but the view of the river below was breathtaking as it tumbled wildly over boulders in its frantic rush toward the valley.

The grassy field next to the school was painted with rainbows of wildflowers. I fancied I could hear the echoes of children playing in its tall grass. Off to one side stood the biggest maple tree I'd ever seen. When I walked closer, I discovered a set of child-sized steps carved into its enormous trunk. I climbed them with care, holding a limb as big as an elephant's leg for support. I trailed my fingers over the initials of students from long ago carved in gnarled bark and imagined their history as I climbed.

About ten feet up, the arms of the tree spread wide. Inside, all but hidden from adult eyes, was a natural platform. Its nearly six-foot diameter must have lured many children over the years, each one convinced they were the first to find it.

Off to one side, a small alcove caught my eye. Stuffed with soft gray-green moss, it was the perfect hidey-hole for tiny hands. I tugged the moss aside and reached inside. There was a rusted metal box. Across the top in a barely visible childish scrawl it read, "Kathleen." I wondered how many years this treasure had waited for the young girl to come back. I tried to pry open the lid but it was rusted shut. I smiled as I tucked it back into the hole again and packed moss around it. Someday, a grown Kathleen might return to find her treasure box still waiting.

The old school was in far better condition than the cabin we had just seen. It would make someone a wonderful home, but we didn't want to rent anymore and I knew somehow, the cabin was meant to be my new home.

When we reached home, John called the owner of the cabin property. He made an offer. It was accepted — that was no surprise — and we arranged to sign the papers.

We could only take our essentials until we built on. Our two older girls were excited about living in the country, but they weren't happy about giving up their belongings, even temporarily. Krista, at nine, was most attached to her possessions. She made a pile of things to take that was half the size of the entire cabin. It was difficult to persuade her that storage wasn't forever. Six-year-old Amber was much easier to reason with. We finally settled on three items for each girl. Autumn, the youngest, wasn't three yet so I chose for her.

As the move drew near, John became just as obsessed with the pioneer concept as I was. Just before moving day, I went into the garage to find two men loading my washer and dryer into their truck. John stood off to the side counting a wad of money.

"What are they doing?" I asked in a panic.

John patted my shoulder. "Calm down. I'm getting rid of all the unnecessary items."

"And how am I supposed to do our laundry, on a rock?"

He smiled and made a small bow as he pointed to an old rusted wringer washer standing up against the back wall.

I discovered later that he also sold my electric range and our portable oil heater. Cooking for five on a woodstove was now a daunting reality.

The day finally came when we said goodbye to our three bedroom, full basement rental. On another rainy Saturday we headed out. John drove a rental truck full of our things and I followed in the station wagon with the girls. Spirits were high as we headed to our new life and home.

Chapter Two

> *I went to the woods because I wished to live deliberately, to front only the essential facts of life, and see if I could not learn what it had to teach, and not, when I come to die, discover that I had not lived...*
>
> — *Henry David Thoreau*
> Walden or Life in the Woods

Excitement turned to despair when we reached the cabin. Unloading the truck in torrential rain and ankle-deep mud took its toll on us as well as our belongings. When the truck was empty, the tiny cabin was bursting with the few things we had brought. Our clothes and hair were matted with mud, Autumn was screaming, the two older girls were arguing, and I was crying from cold and exhaustion. We stood in a steaming huddle, surrounded by towers of soggy boxes while the excess water ran back outside through the holes in the floor.

"Enough!" John shouted. "The first thing we need is a fire." The only problem was, in all our careful planning, we had neglected to bring a supply of wood. I watched as this fact registered on John's face. "Okay, you two girls go outside and find a few sticks. Sal, shut that baby up. I'll have a look at the stove."

Krista and Amber shuffled out the door to do as they were told. At least it had stopped raining for the moment. I could hear Amber muttering as they left. "I don't like this country. It isn't very fun here."

I quieted Autumn by sticking a cracker in her mouth and watched as John unwrapped some things from a box and stuffed the stove with paper. The girls came trooping in, their arms loaded with soggy sticks. I handed them a couple of towels and we all gathered around the stove to wait for the heat.

John struck a match and held it to the paper. Within seconds the entire cabin was full of thick white smoke. Coughing and choking, we were forced back outside. John had started the fire with the damper shut. With the chimney and both doors open we were able to go back in to start drying out before we froze.

That night, dinner was scorched scrambled eggs and burnt toast. I had faith I would get the hang of cooking on the woodstove eventually, but it sure wasn't that night. By bedtime, there were wall-to-wall mattresses on the floor with stacks of boxes shoved together in the center to form a makeshift wall. Still, it was like sleeping in a wooden tent. There was little room to walk. John would have to build on soon.

Trips to the smelly outhouse got old quickly. John rigged up an inside pot I could take out and empty. I noticed he didn't volunteer to empty it.

The next day, the rental truck had to be taken back. When we returned at midday the sun was shining. I decided the girls would feel better about their new home if we walked to the river, so we spent several hours roaming before the rain came again.

Monday morning, after we'd been there a week, things were already starting to fall into a routine. John left for his job about thirty miles away and the school bus picked up the two older girls. Autumn and I were left in the wilderness with no car and no telephone. Isolated again, a feeling I hadn't counted on. The first thing we always did was to check the fire. One glance at the woodbin told me it was time to find more sticks. I would be glad when summer got here. The small cabin drew moisture like a sponge. When the fire went out it was colder inside than out.

So out we went. Autumn and I bundled up to traipse through the forest gathering sticks. It was a misty morning and we were on a different trail searching for a new supply of wood. The trees were almost leafed out in their summer green, making lovely patterns across the path. It seemed as though we were walking under yards of black lace.

The trees might be getting ready for summer but it was still chilly so I was wearing an old fur coat the girls had fondly named "Kitty." My arms were loaded with wood and Autumn trailed slightly behind, singing happy songs softly to herself. Then I rounded the bend in the trail and stopped cold. Back in the shadows, where the trail rose to the levee road, stood the huge shape of a man. By his side was a smaller, lighter shape. I heard Autumn come up behind me. None of us moved. From the shadows they appeared to be watching us just like we were watching them. The only things I could see were their eyes: enormous round eyes with a slightly greenish cast. *Full of knowledge, those eyes.* Although I felt no threat, a shiver touched my spine. The thought came to me that I had seen those eyes before... somewhere, sometime. The large one cocked his head, with a questioning look. *I wonder if he's curious about my fur coat.* His movement brought me back to reality and I whispered to Autumn. "Turn around honey and walk, don't run."

Turning, I dropped my load of sticks, grabbed her arm, and propelled her slowly back the way we had come. When the two figures were no longer in sight, I picked Autumn up and ran for home where we crawled into bed and stayed for the rest of the day.

When John came home he was furious that there was no wood. I had no excuse for why Autumn and I had spent the day in bed and stammered something about not feeling well. John slammed out the door and I thought back to earlier in the day, but all I could remember was walking a short way down a path. It was a long time before I remembered meeting the creatures and I still don't recall how I got back to the cabin.

Although the road had appeared deserted when we first drove it, the sound of dogs barking told me there were houses somewhere nearby. That was a comforting feeling in case of an emergency.

Autumn and I gathered sticks for several more weeks until one morning a truck backed into the driveway and two men began pitching big, beautiful chunks of firewood into a pile.

"Your husband wanted to surprise you," one of the men said.

Tears rolled down my face as I began stacking wood.

I was becoming more adept at using the cook stove. My biscuits were much less like hockey pucks and burnt offerings were a thing of the past. I had always been a good cook on an electric range but woodstoves take some doing.

The girls loved their new school. They looked forward to catching the bus each morning. John still had friends at work that he spent time with. I had never made any women friends in town. With three children to care for, it seemed there was never time. Autumn was good company but I longed for a woman to share my thoughts with. There were a lot of things that interested me that I couldn't talk to John about. I would start to talk about something out of the ordinary and it was like he couldn't even hear me.

One day in late spring, I was outside getting an armload of wood when I noticed someone in the cabin with the boarded up windows. Long dark hair and a round beaming face appeared in the open doorway.

"Hi," I said, "I'm Sali. Can I help you?"

"Oh, no thanks, sometimes this old fire is a booger-bear to start but I think I've got it now."

"No. I meant who are you? Nobody lives over here." I said.

"Oh. This is my cabin. I'm Youtle Tum Tum. In Chinook, it means Joy. You can call me Youdi. I was just getting my grill started. I caught a dandy salmon this morning and I'm going to cook it. Care to join me?"

Her presence, her chatter, the thought of having a neighbor — I felt a bit overwhelmed. "What did you say your name is?"

"Youtle Tum Tum. Just call me Youdi, it's easier. Would you like some fish when it's done? It's too big to eat alone. Of course,

I'll take some over to Emily and the boys but they're never that hungry." She gestured over her shoulder with her thumb. I saw no one. "Emily Ann is my daughter. Haven't you met? She lives over there with her family."

"No," I said. "I haven't met any of the neighbors. I've been busy settling in. I didn't know anyone lived over there either."

"Ah," Youdi smiled knowingly, "City folks. Well, don't worry. You'll figure it all out. Burned any biscuits yet?"

I laughed, "Quite a few, actually."

Youdi looked up and pointed to my chest. She looked at me sharply with dark eyes. "That's an interesting pendant you're wearing. Do you know where it came from?"

I told her that my mother had bought it in an Indian trading post in Arizona, when she was a young woman.

"Well, what goes around, comes around," Youdi muttered.

I watched as she plucked a small leather pouch from beneath

Youdi's cabin

her jacket, tucked some of the green sprigs it held into the belly of the giant fish, and then placed a rusted cover over the grill.

"Have you learned to make coffee yet? I could use a cup."

I laughed. "That I can do pretty well."

We sat with our coffee and made small talk. That was how I began the closest friendship I've ever had with another woman. In the months ahead, Youdi and I would rarely be apart. Her earthiness and straight talk added a dimension to my life I had never known. I could talk to Youdi about anything and not surprise her. She never judged me.

Later that day, Youdi introduced me to her daughter, Emily Ann, and her two small boys. Emily was so shy she was nearly invisible. She spoke only in monosyllables and only when spoken to. Her long, straight, black hair and huge, soulful eyes reminded me of Keen paintings from the 1960s. Her two boys were tiny versions of their mother. I had never been around such quiet children. It was no wonder I hadn't known they lived next door. Greg, the eldest, was just Autumn's age. Randy was a baby, still in diapers.

Greg and Autumn bonded instantly. They played that day in the sandbox John had built from an old waterbed frame. We all ate Youdi's salmon for lunch. It was the best fish I had ever tasted.

Youdi lived about an hour's drive away in Tacoma with her husband, Bud. The cabin was Youdi's retreat from the white man's world. After that day she came often. She seemed as hungry for my companionship as I was for hers. I wondered if Bud minded her frequent absences for days at a time. He never came with her.

As spring turned to summer, Youdi became a fixture next door. She was a puzzle to me. Though she was a mature woman with children almost my age, all the ages of woman and girl came together in her personality. At times she was a playful child, showing wonder at the simple beauty of nature, then the next moment she would utter a remark so sage I would be completely taken aback.

Together with Emily and the three small children, Youdi and I walked many miles that first summer. I learned a lot about my forest home. Wherever we went, Youdi carried her gathering bag. As she gathered bark, roots, and herbs, she became Youdi the teacher and explained their uses.

"Boneset, or comfrey," chimed Youdi in her high, singsong voice, "is useful for broken bones. If you wilt the leaves and use them as a compress, the break will heal much faster. In the past, the root was mixed with bear grease and used as an ointment to

Emily's cabin

heal wounds. Nowadays, Vaseline is much easier to come by than bear fat and it smells better. It's the comfrey that does the healing." Then off she'd go down the path, tucking her harvest into her bag, her voice trailing behind her.

"When an Indian had a headache, he chewed a piece of willow bark. That's where aspirin comes from." Youdi peeled off a generous strip and added it to her collection.

The days of that summer passed easily. Most of the time Emily and her boys preferred their own company and Autumn sometimes stayed with them to play. On the days when my other two girls spent time at a friend's, Youdi and I tramped the woods together. We must have made a comical pair; she was short and dark, I was a foot taller with blonde streaked hair almost to my waist.

One day, we found a deep pool at the river. As we sat eating our lunch, a huge bird flew from the ridge, circled us, and faded into the distance. This one didn't disappear. I told Youdi about my experience on the first day here. She didn't comment then, but later I caught her looking at me with an odd expression. Finally she spoke.

"When I was a child, my grandmother told me the legend of the blue heron. Since then I have always watched for one that disappears. It is said that he brings a message from the spirit world to the one who sees him. You have been chosen, Sal. It's a great honor. The day will come when the message will be clear to you."

A feeling like warm water spread over me. Those words would echo into my future.

During that first summer, I met another unusual neighbor. I walked out to pick up the mail one day and saw a squat woman moving rapidly toward me on the road. Her purple and orange outfit would have been visible on a moonless night. She had gray-black hair that stood up in tufts above a pink headband. Pulling her along was the most hideous dog I had ever seen. It appeared to be suffering from mange, and losing badly. Its fur was missing in great clumps. The little fur that was left looked suspiciously like the tufts sprouting from the woman's headband.

They trotted toward me at an alarming pace. Just when the dog threatened to run me over, the woman gave a neck-breaking tug and gagged it to a stop. "Whoa, Black Jack! Whoa!." The dog hacked like it was dying, but continued to lunge in my direction, growling. "Don't worry about Black Jack, honey," the woman wheezed. "He's blind as a bat and deaf as a post. His nose still works some, but even if he could find you he can't bite. Ain't got no teeth."

When the woman snorted I noticed she had left her teeth at home as well.

"You must be the new kid on the block. What's your name, girl?"

"Uh, Sali." I said, looking for a way to escape.

"Well, Shelly, nice to meet you. Gets right lonesome out here. Come on over sometime and we'll chew the fat. I can tell you some things about these parts that'll curl your hair."

She turned abruptly and headed in the direction from which she'd come.

“Oh yeah,” she said, over her shoulder, “the name’s Esther. Gotta go. Got me a hot game of bingo in Enumclaw tonight.” Off she went, Black Jack dragging her back down the road.

I chuckled as I walked to the cabin. I had never met anyone who spoke in clichés before. I pictured Esther in her youth, dancing the jitterbug, flung over some sailor’s shoulder, exposing her embroidered underwear marked “Tuesday” on a Friday night. She may even have been beautiful in her day. Now she was a spring flower gone to seed.

Chapter Three

At first it seemed a little speck,
And then it seemed a mist;
It moved and moved, and took at last
A certain shape, I wist.

— Samuel Taylor Coleridge
"The Rime of the Ancient Mariner"

I heard a knock on my door. I assumed it was Youdi and I yelled, "Come in." When I turned around, a smiling Esther stood next to me. Today she had teeth, pearly white, but ill-fitting. Once again, she was dressed like the lone survivor of a thrift store explosion.

"Mornin' Sheryl," Esther clicked at me. "You never came by for a chat, so I came here. I left my dog home so we could set a spell."

"Oh great," I thought. Autumn stood at Esther's knee. She seemed fascinated by the sound Esther's teeth made when she talked. I drew her aside and whispered, "Go outside and play."

Esther took Autumn's departure as a sign to begin our chat. "Have you heard them screams the last couple a nights?"

"Screams?" I shook my head, puzzled. I'd had the TV on late.

"I thought not, so I come by to fill you in. All the dogs been goin' nuts. Black Jack's been hidin' under my bed. He can't hear them but he can smell that garbage smell. Some folks claim the screams is the ghosts of them Chinamen that got killed in the mine cave-in back in the early days. Buried them alive, it did. Never even tried to get them out when they found out they wasn't white. Just closed up that mine an' let them rot. Then, other folks says them screams is that Bigfoot monster the Injuns used to talk about. I'm partial to the Bigfoot tale myself."

I blanched, both at the subject matter and at Esther's racial epithets. God, I was glad I'd sent Autumn out to play but now I could see her coming back up the path.

"Uh... Esther, I hate to cut this short, but my daughter's coming back. We have to go into town. I'm sure you understand."

"Oh, sure. Well, it's been nice talkin' to you, Sue. I'll see you again, real soon."

Later, I was still thinking about Esther's story, especially the garbage smell, when I heard Youdi's car pull in next door. I hurried over to talk to her. We laughed together when I described Esther's outfit, but Youdi grew strangely quiet when I told her about the screams Esther described. That's when I knew she'd heard them, too.

"Talk to me, Youdi. You're giving me the creeps. I thought she was just a loony old lady, but she's not making this up, is she?"

Youdi took a deep breath and looked into my eyes from under her thick, dark lashes. "My people have always known of Bigfoot — we called them *Skookum*. Before the white man came we shared the forest with them. I've never seen one, but I know they exist. I haven't spoken to you of Skookum because I felt one day you would question me. That would be the time to tell you. You're my friend, Sal, but you are also a *pasaiook*... a white person. White people do not comprehend that Skookum are sacred beings. They hunt them, to kill one, so that they can prove they exist. They may as well hunt the wind." She paused, thoughtful. "Even though you are *pasaiook* now, I believe this was not always so and may not be so again. The heron has paid you a visit."

"But I haven't heard any screams."

"I have a feeling you will, my friend. Know that you have nothing to fear."

When she said that, it was like opening the door to memories that were usually hidden. My thoughts went back to my first day in the valley. "Come inside. There's something I need to tell you."

As we sat at the kitchen table I told Youdi about the shape I'd glimpsed on the trail behind her cabin and how, after running a ways, it had disappeared like the heron. "Whatever it was left behind a bit of hair on a limb. Wait here and I'll find it."

While I was in the bedroom, rummaging through unpacked boxes, I could hear Youdi tinkering in the kitchen. When I emerged, she handed me a cup of fragrant tea. She reached out and took the tiny bit of hair from my hand.

"Aiyee," she whispered. "This came from the one who disappeared?"

I nodded.

Youdi took a small leather pouch from her pocket and withdrew what looked like dried herbs. She sprinkled these in our cups. "This is a special gift. Keep it with you always. It has great power. Sit, and I will tell you the legend of Skookum, as told to me by my grandmother.

"Once, long ago, a warlike tribe swept down from the mountains to attack a neighboring village. Their fierce warriors slaughtered many of the people and forced the survivors to flee into the forest. These people finally made their way to an island where they could live in safety. Over the years they developed a form of self-hypnosis that enabled them to see in the dark. They also found the power to become invisible to those who were not a part of their tribe. Slowly, they evolved into a different kind of being. Only their peaceful manner remained the same.

"With the passing years they grew in size and strength and became covered with long hair over most of their bodies. They taught themselves to mimic the animals of the forest and learned how to make the many other sounds they heard once they left their island home. They became Skookum, who would come to be known by all tribes, but by different names. Grandmother said Skookum were glimpsed often before the *pasaiook* came. These giants lived side by side with our people. When the whites came, slaughtering the Indian, Skookum moved deep into the forest. The few who come back still have the ability to disappear if they feel threatened. The only thing these giants never could control was the smell that accompanied this act. The thing you surprised on the trail..."

Youdi's words seemed to come from a great distance...

I found myself standing on a path in the forest with an herb bag slung over my shoulder. A strange whistling filled the air. As if of their own accord, my moccasins began to follow the notes deeper into the woods.

No matter how far I went, the tune was just a little farther on, or to the side of me. This in itself served to increase my curiosity; the whistling was the only sound I could hear. Never before had the forest been so silent. The melody was repeated every few seconds, as if to make sure I did not lose interest.

My herb gathering long forgotten, I realized I was in a place I had never been before. I must have followed the sounds a long way. I had grown up in these woods and I did not think there was a part of the area unknown to me.

Never once had I caught sight of the creature from which the haunting melody came. It was unlike anything I had ever heard. Once or twice I caught a glimpse of a shadow in the underbrush ahead, and several times I heard heavy footfalls. It seemed to be leading me to a certain spot.

Eventually I came to a clear stream surrounded by tall ferns and wildflowers. I glanced in the direction from which I had heard the last notes and there on the other side of the stream stood a misty brown form. At first I couldn't bring it into focus: it was the same color as the tree trunks where it stood. Then it stepped forward and I was looking into the biggest eyes I had ever seen. The beast might have been big and hairy, but the eyes were unmistakably human.

The next thing I knew, I was back at the kitchen table with Youdi. She was smiling smugly. “Boy, what did you put in that tea?” I asked.

“Just some harmless herbs from the forest. Your journey was not my doing.”

After Youdi left, I sat and thought about what had happened. I hadn’t even mentioned my woolgathering, but she had known. I was sure it hadn’t been a dream; it had been too real. I remembered feeling the damp forest floor through my moccasins as I followed the whistling, but I had never worn moccasins in my life. I pictured the eyes I’d seen. Old as time and full of wisdom, they had been gentle and kind.

That night I heard the screams.

I was jolted awake by a woman-like cry that echoed off the ridge across the river. The neighboring dogs went crazy, barking and whining pitifully. Another answering scream sounded in the distance.

I crept through the living room and opened the door to the back deck. No one stirred in the house but me. I stepped outside and shut the door.

The next scream split the still night air like an axe. It spoke to a part of my brain, an ancient part of my mind, where forgotten memories lived. Deep in my soul I felt the time of change. The sound bounced back and forth across the valley floor until a new one took its place. Shivers ran like electricity down my arms. When the wind stirred my hair, it held the first hint of fall.

When I walked outside the next morning, a thin layer of frost covered the woods. Wood smoke and fir mingled with the pungent scent of the herbs Youdi had planted alongside the cabin. Through the pantry window, rows of wild strawberry and blackberry preserves shone like bottled jewels. The smell of baking bread wafted through the still morning air like a crooked finger, beckoning me inside to breakfast.

No longer did I make daily trips to the market for groceries; the nearest store was almost thirty miles away. Now, major grocery shopping happened once a month, if we didn't have it, we went without. Life was so much simpler here. John's chicken coop and rabbit hutches were out back, so we had eggs and meat. The next summer I planned to plant a small garden.

I had become part of this life. I knew that if we ever had to leave, something inside me would die. From the first day this place felt like a missing part of me and now I was whole. And now, with last night's screams still echoing in my mind, I felt a thrill. Something significant, important, was happening here and it had only just begun.

Chapter Four

For here the religion that languishes in crowded cities or steals shamefaced to hide itself in dim churches, flourishes greatly, filling the soul with a solemn joy. Face to face with nature on the vast hills of eventide, who does not feel himself close to the unseen?

— W. H. Hudson
"The Purple Land"

Autumn was jumping with excitement. This was the day we were going shopping for John's birthday present. He had recently bought an old truck to drive to work, so I had the station wagon. Although most days it sat in our driveway, I now had a car to go with our newly installed phone in case of emergency.

Our destination was the B&I department store in Tacoma. In addition to being well stocked, it also had a full-sized carousel inside.

The drive into town was like a Currier and Ives painting of fall come to life. Fields stood ready for harvest, the tall grain moving like ocean waves in the crisp breeze. The Puyallup valley was a sea of flower farms with rows of spent tulip and daffodil plants waiting to be clipped. Larkspur and mums still bloomed profusely, as if daring Nature to do her worst. In the truck gardens, bright orange pumpkins dotted the brown earth, waiting patiently for Halloween to come.

Few cars were in the parking lot of the B&I that early morning. We entered the store from the rear and walked toward the men's clothing section. I had just taken a flannel shirt from the rack when a vaguely familiar odor reached my nostrils. I was catapulted back to my first day in the valley.

The clothing racks and the sounds of shopping dissolved. Instead, I was running for my life down a sandy trail in the forest, pursued by a mysterious beast.

Sali and Autumn and the station wagon

Then the flashback was gone. The odor, however, remained. I sniffed in all directions, trying to determine where the scent was coming from. It was so out of place. Sweat poured from my face, and my breath came in short gasps.

Then I realized its source.

I grabbed Autumn's hand and we raced to the back wall of the store. The odor became more pungent as we neared a large glassed-in cage built into the wall. A sign read, "My Name is Ivan."

I choked when the gorilla's eyes met mine. We stared at each other through the thick glass. He looked so intelligent I expected him to speak. Sorrow overwhelmed me as I watched him move listlessly in his small prison. When I looked at Autumn, her eyes were filled with tears, too.

My heart ached as I imagined the day he was captured. Then I thought of the Skookum legend that Youdi had told me. She'd said they couldn't control the odor that occurred when they disappeared or were threatened. This creature didn't have the powers of Skookum. He would live his life on display in this box.

We left the store without buying anything or riding the carousel. I felt sick. I bought Autumn an ice cream cone instead and purchased John's present elsewhere.

On the way home I thought about the gorilla. Somewhere I had read that it was less than a hundred years ago when the first gorilla was captured, proving to science they existed. Before that, there were only rumors of people seeing giant man-like beasts in the jungle. Now, thanks to man, their species was near extinction. I vowed then that no harm would come to Skookum through me.

John's birthday dinner went well but Autumn and I didn't eat much. I couldn't get the picture of that gorilla out of my mind. John asked me several times what was wrong. Finally I told him. He laughed.

"That animal was probably born in a cage and knows nothing else. You girls are such softies."

I didn't believe the gorilla had been born in captivity. I had seen the hopeless look in his eyes.

I felt the need of some freedom myself. I sneaked out the back door for a short walk. Dark was coming earlier as fall settled in. Birds twittered in the chill air, making their preparations for the night. Walking soberly down the path, I came upon two deer. When they saw me, they stood like brown statues, not ten feet ahead. We gazed at each other for what seemed like forever before they relaxed and went back to grazing. A light mist began to fall as I watched them feed.

This was a rare treat for a former city girl like me. Being close to wild creatures was still too new to take for granted. I studied the doe at great length. Her huge, innocent eyes seemed to beckon me closer, and I obliged. Keeping a careful eye on the buck for any sign of objection, I inched forward... one step at a time, until my hand was only inches from her muzzle.

The buck was several feet back in the underbrush. His antlers glistened with moisture, and his breath came in short bursts of steam. He watched my progress with rounded eyes, but was much more tolerant of my approach than I had expected.

When the doe put her nose to my outstretched hand, the spell was broken. The buck squatted down to pee then let out a snort of steam in her direction. She obeyed, instantly going to his side. They walked off together toward the river.

I stumbled back to the cabin in a daze. As I reached the steps, the air was pierced with a prolonged scream. I hastily made my way inside.

During the night, I woke and went to the kitchen for a drink. The cloud cover and fine mist of early evening had given way to a clear sky and a glorious moon, sitting high over the ridge. Among the trees at the end of the path, I thought I caught a glimpse of something moving. I blinked and rubbed my eyes, but a dark shape continued its slow progress upriver. Tiny lights blinked as they moved between trees. My first thought was that it was fireflies... *But there are no fireflies in the Northwest,* I remembered. The lights were concentrated around the moving shape, as though lighting its way.

On impulse, I tapped my fingernail loudly on the window. The lights went out and the shape stopped moving. The forest was still. I waited a few minutes before going back to bed but saw nothing more.

Several weeks went by before Youdi could break loose from her home in the city again and spend time at the river. By the time I saw her again, I had almost forgotten the gorilla and the creature with the lights.

When Youdi stepped out of her car, she had the compressed energy of a bear freed from a cage. Her first words were abrupt.

"What has happened here while I was gone?"

"Well, 'hello' to you, too. A lot happened on John's birthday, then not much since."

"Begin at the beginning," she ordered.

"Tell you what, smiling woman," I grinned, sarcastically. "I'll let you read it for yourself while I make coffee." I handed her the journal I'd started.

Youdi read through the notes with barely a nod of her head but when she looked up there were tears in her eyes.

"It doesn't matter that you are not an Indian, your heart is one with our people. No wild creature should be put in a cage to be gawked at. Every living thing was put on this earth by the Great Spirit to be free. When I was a girl, I had pets, but they were free to come and go as they pleased. Our people hunted for necessity, not for sport. You have that same respect for all creatures."

The more time I spent with Youdi, the more her Native ways seemed practical... even familiar. This didn't seem to surprise her, but John was puzzled by the changes in me. One day, after he got back from an evening in town with his buddies, he looked at me and fingered one of my braids.

"What are you doing, turning into a damned squaw?"

I recoiled from his touch. I didn't like his tone of voice nor his offensive language. In fact, I was starting to like any time with John less and less. He was surly and distant when he drank and he'd been staying in town after work with his buddies a lot in the past few weeks.

The times with Youdi were good, though. When Youdi and I went gathering, I no longer needed coaching to recognize plants.

One day I even surprised myself. I was kneeling to strip the flowers from a dried stalk when Youdi came silently to my side.

"What is that you have there?" She asked in her musical way.

"Mullein. Isn't it beautiful? I'll use it for tea for coughs and colds this winter." I looked up into Youdi's eyes when I realized what I'd said. She smiled back.

"So, the student has become the teacher. Mullein was to be your next lesson. But it seems you already know its uses. How can that be?" she teased.

She was right. I had even known the right time to harvest it. That information, and much more, seemed to be seeping from some hidden spring in my mind.

One weekend in early October, John butchered our first batch of rabbits, all but a couple of breeding pairs. He had never done this before but someone at work had told him how to kill and skin them. My job would be to cut and wrap them for the freezer.

John quickly did what was necessary, then brought the still-warm carcasses in to soak in cold water while he went back out to clean up. I saw him drop a bundle of hides wrapped in plastic on the porch. "I'll be back soon to show you how to cut up the rabbits," he yelled as he left.

I grabbed my sharpest knife, said a short prayer of thanks to the spirits of the rabbits for giving their lives so that we could live, and chanted softly as I began cutting.

When I had the meat neatly stored away, I retrieved the hides and scraped off the fat clinging to the inside of each one. Then I rubbed salt into the underside and rolled each hide into a neat cylinder lined with cedar bark I had already stripped and pounded. I would change this as it became moist. I was finishing the last hide when John returned.

"Now, I'll show you how to cut up those... Hey, where's all the rabbits?"

"I cut them up. They're in the freezer." He looked puzzled. "Where are the hides? You didn't throw them away, did you? I'm going to nail them on boards, then make something out of them after they dry."

I pointed to the stack of cylinders behind the stove. "They're back there. Drying them on a board would make them hard and brittle. They'd be useless. This way, they'll dry slowly. If I change the bark often, they'll be soft." He looked at me like I'd grown another head.

"How the hell do you know that?"

It was a fair question. I'd never even eaten rabbit before, much less tanned a hide.

"Uh... I must have read it somewhere."

I watched John slam out the door. He re-wrapped the rabbit guts in paper and plastic and rattled the trashcans excessively as he secured the lids. We'd had quite a problem with animals dumping our trash, so he hooked the lids with bungee cords until dump day.

That night, I was awakened by the clattering of metal at about 2:00 a.m. I could hear odd sounds, like a group of people speaking Chinese. I hesitated to wake my snoring husband and instead slipped silently from bed. I tiptoed to the window overlooking the trashcans. The yard light was off but a full moon lit up the yard. Then the shadow of what appeared to be a huge man passed between the moon and me. When I gasped, I got a whiff of the smell I knew well. I couldn't breathe as I watched the shape fade into the trees.

John woke first in the morning. "Damn dogs. I'll kill every one of them."

I struggled awake and threw on my robe. Outside, a scene of utter destruction met my eyes. Trashcans had been thrown like toys around the yard. One was flattened. Their contents had been dumped into a large pile. John was cursing and filling new garbage bags. I came up beside him, putting my hand on his arm, "John?"

He shook himself free. "Leave me alone. I've got to clean up this mess. Smells like a skunk's been here too."

"Don't you notice anything unusual about all this?"

"All I know is I'm gonna shoot some dogs."

"No. Stop, and look closer. No animal I know unties a bag. They rip it to shreds. All those carefully wrapped rabbit guts have been carefully *un*wrapped." I showed him a stack of papers spread out on a rock. "What kind of animal unhooks bungee cords, or flattens a trash can?"

"So, what did all this, garbage burglars?" He sneered. "Oh, I get it, Bigfoot. Is that what you're getting at? Give me a break. There's no such thing. I suppose that's what left this big pile of shit over here. Maybe I should scoop it up and save it for your friend, Youdi."

I didn't like his attitude, but I took a chance and told John what I'd seen last night. His expression went from skeptical to serious.

"You know, maybe you're right. I've seen some pretty strange things myself lately."

"You have?" I felt a glimmer of hope. Maybe I could trust John after all.

"Yeah, last week when I was walking near the river this huge thing came floating down the channel. It had a head the size of a Volkswagen and a neck about twenty feet long. At first I was afraid, but then I realized it was lost. I crept up real close and gave it directions back to Scotland." At the look on my face, John doubled over with laughter. "You'd better watch who you tell your Bigfoot stories to. Ever since you started hanging around with that damn Indian you've been acting weird."

I turned and stalked back inside. So much for confiding in my husband. He could pick up the garbage himself.

Later, it occurred to me that I should have saved a sample from the big pile of droppings. After John left for the dump, I went out to retrieve some, but he had cleaned that up as well.

The next day, October 20, was Autumn's third birthday. While John was gone, I put a cake in the oven, then wrote down the events of the night before. The fact that I couldn't discuss any of these things with John really irked me. Apparently, none of the rest of my family had heard or seen anything. John had smelled the odor in the yard, but he assumed it was a skunk. I longed to talk to Youdi, but I couldn't afford to call long distance every time something happened.

There was a loud knock on the door; Esther burst in before I could answer. Her outfit lit the room. Blackjack wasn't with her. "Afternoon, Shelly. I just came by to see if you heard all that ruckus last night. Sounded like someone was gettin' done in over here. You and your man wasn't fightin', was you? Oh, what a purty cake. You havin' a party?"

"Uh... yes Esther. It's Autumn's birthday."

Just then, John walked in. Esther's eyes grew wide and she patted the plastic flowers in her hair. "Whoo-eee. Sarah didn't tell me what a looker you was. It's about time I met her better half. I'm Esther. I just came over to see what all that noise was last night. Like to scared me to death." She batted her eyes like she had sand in them.

John smiled weakly and inched away from her. He was saved from Esther's advances by another knock at the door. Emily and her two boys entered.

We all gathered around to sing the birthday song. Autumn proudly blew out her candles as Esther bellowed out the last line. "HAPPY BIIIRTHDAAAAY, DEEEEAR ARTHURRRRR... happy birthday to yooou." She elbowed John in the ribs. "Arthur's a funny name for a little girl, Gerald."

Autumn opened her gifts with the frantic glee of a three year old. The boys had bought her a new shovel and pail. Youdi made her a totem pole with faces of the sacred spirits. John and I had bought her the "Dapper Dan" doll she had wanted for so long. Both her sisters had made her cards with pictures of things she liked. Then Esther stepped forward and handed Autumn a beautiful blue-gray feather. She stared at it in childish wonder. It was the wing feather from a blue heron.

That night, the dreams began.

I awoke covered in sweat and out of breath, as if I'd been running. I had the feeling I'd frantically been searching for someone. I couldn't remember who, but I knew I'd failed to find them. I slipped out of bed and sat on the couch under the big living room window for a long time. The night was silent. Shapes and snatches of conversation from my dream lurked at the edges of my memory. The harder I tried to bring them into focus, the further away they danced. A sense of urgency prevented sleep. There was something I needed to do. In my waking state the dream hung just out of reach, foggy and elusive as a wisp of smoke.

I curled up in the corner of the couch like a sow bug and managed to put aside the fragments of my dream quest, then fell deeply asleep.

I awoke to the bustle of morning. The aftereffects of my dream were pushed to the background as I helped the girls get ready for school. When Autumn and I were alone, we took a walk to the river. I needed to clear my head and reflect on last night's experience.

Autumn stumped along beside me but my mind was elsewhere. We were walking up river on the levee road when I saw a flash of bright light out over the water, then a heron circled lazily over the same spot. He dove to pluck a fish from the water, then rose majestically into the sky, and was... *gone.*

"Where'd he go, Mom?"

Autumn's question startled me. "You mean you saw him too?"

She nodded. We stood hand in hand watching the sky before heading home. I wondered what Youdi would make of this.

That night I fell asleep on the couch. When I woke, I was fully dressed and my shoes were wet. I was becoming concerned. If I were sleepwalking alone in the forest, I could be hurt or lost. I hadn't told John what was happening; he was barely speaking to me these days. I tried to call Youdi several times that day, but there was no answer.

The dreams came again that night. I woke sweaty and shaking. This was scary. Visions of faces and voices speaking in an unfamiliar tongue flitted through my mind. The essence of wood smoke hung in my nostrils and my legs ached as if I'd traveled a great distance. I was afraid to go back to sleep, but I must have, because when I struggled to the surface again the sounds of morning engulfed me.

John was grumbling because he had to make his own coffee. The older girls were racing out the door to catch the bus. I was so groggy my eyes began to close again. I was drifting off when a small voice jolted me awake. "Wake up Mom, I'm hungry."

I stumbled to the kitchen to fix Autumn a bowl of cereal as John slammed out the door. When Autumn was settled, I made my way to the bedroom to put on dry shoes and socks. I sat on the frame of the waterbed and happened to glance at my reflection in the old mirror on the dresser. The watery depths of the glass seemed to shimmer. God, I looked awful. I blinked my eyes to focus, but when I looked again the face that looked back at me wasn't mine.

My sharp intake of breath brought a lopsided smile to the face of the old Indian in the mirror. Then the smile faded. Ancient eyes looked into mine. The expression of wisdom and sadness was so deep I couldn't look away. I felt the past ripple across my mind.

From a face written over with countless wrinkles, black eyes beckoned. His long, braided hair was pure white. It hung over his shoulder, ending in a leather thong. Three blue-gray feathers decorated the end; much like the one Esther had given Autumn.

I sat suspended in time until Autumn called my name. When I looked back, he was gone. I sat motionless, trying to get my bearings. What was happening to me?

I ran to the phone and called Youdi. She answered on the first ring. The events of the last few days poured from my mouth. For some reason, I left out the part about seeing the old Indian in the mirror. I wasn't sure if I even believed that one myself.

"Don't be afraid of your dreams." Youdi said. "Everything has a purpose. One day soon it will all become clear."

I felt better after talking with Youdi. Her words of wisdom seemed to settle my nerves. Maybe it was the fact that I could share these things with someone who understood. She told me to look upon my dreams as a learning experience — then the messages would come through.

Chapter Five

The old Man still stood talking by my side;
But now his voice to me was like a stream
Scarce heard; nor word from word could I divide;
And the whole body of the Man did seem
Like one whom I had met with in a dream;

— William Wordsworth
"The Leech-Gatherer"

I didn't dream for several nights, but each time I passed my dresser I thought about the old man staring back at me. I began to wonder if I had even seen him at all.

A couple of nights later, I heard screams in the distance but nothing significant happened.

Youdi didn't come out again until November 8th, my birthday. Early in the morning, I heard a soft knocking on the door. When I opened it, she thrust a gaily-wrapped package into my hand. "Happy birthday, Sal. Let's walk to the river and you can open your gift."

It was a mild fall day. Maple leaves drifted on the breeze like large yellow butterflies. Autumn kicked her way gleefully through the thick carpet, leaving a colorful wake behind her. A thin, blue wisp of smoke from one of the neighboring houses drifted across the trail. Indian summer would be over soon and winter on its way.

"Open your gift," Youdi said with a sly grin.

When I tore away the hand-painted paper, a curious sight met my eyes. Woven into a ring of sticks was a lacy macramé made of twine. Suspended here and there between the holes were colorful glass beads in the shapes of animals. A delicate tracing of beads and feathers hung from the bottom. It was somehow familiar, yet not. Youdi saw my puzzled expression and explained. "It's a dream catcher. Do you know what it's for?"

I shook my head.

"Legend has it that the good dreams pass through the center hole to the sleeping person. The bad dreams are trapped in the web, where they perish in the light of dawn. It will help protect you in the nights to come."

My eyes filled. "Thank you, Youdi. It's beautiful."

That night, John noticed my gift hanging above the bed. "What in the hell is that?"

I explained the legend to him.

"You don't really believe that crap, do you? That little squaw's got you headed toward the deep end. Don't make me sorry we moved here." He turned away and went to sleep.

The rains came again that night and so did the dreams. I awoke around 3:00 a.m. and lay staring at the bedroom ceiling with half-shut eyes. This time the dream had been pleasant, that much I knew. When I tried to recall the details, all I could remember was walking in the forest. The rest was like a shape in the darkness: no sooner glimpsed, than gone.

I rose and went to the living room. Sitting in the dark, I gazed out the picture window John had installed. Gray-bellied clouds hung low and the rain came down like bullets against the glass, but it was warm and dry in our cabin. Unable to sleep, my mind drifted.

With the coming of foul weather, I always felt a sense of urgency, as if I should check our provisions to make sure we had enough to last through the hard months ahead. I'd been told the power went out a lot here. Over the last few months, John had swallowed his pride and made several improvements to the cabin. We now had a real wood heater and an ample supply of firewood. It was much better than heating with the cook stove.

He had also bought me another electric range at a secondhand store. Using lumber from a demolished house nearby, he had built on a bedroom for us and two smaller ones for the girls. Currently, he was working on a big bathroom that would not only have a tub and toilet, but room for a washer and dryer.

My life was comfortable, except for John's attitude. As time went on, he became more cranky and remote. The girls began avoiding him whenever possible, as did Youdi. John's dislike of her and her Native ways was obvious. She came when John was at work or off elsewhere. When she stayed at her cabin, I went there or to Emily's.

As fingers of mist wrapped themselves in a ghostly embrace around our cabin and my thoughts, I fell asleep on the couch.

Morning crept its way through the fog and I awoke with a kink in my neck. After getting the kids ready for school, I used my electric range to brown a pot roast for dinner and my wandering thoughts continued, as if uninterrupted by a night's sleep. My mind went to Youdi and how many things she had taught me. Our gathering expeditions had turned my pantry into an herbalist's delight. I could now cure many of my family's ailments without the aid of a doctor.

Youdi had fed my hunger for the unknown as well. I remembered her telling me that nearly every country on earth has mysteries that are discounted as mere legends because they don't conform to the ideas of the scientists and scholars who are in power. All Native American tribes have legends of their origins. These histories have been passed down through generations of fathers and sons. When white men reached America, it seemingly never occurred to them that the tribes they encountered were the remnants of lost civilizations.

The Hopi tribe claimed that their ancestors, the Anasazi, who built the amazing cliff dwellings at Mesa Verde in Arizona, came to this world through a hole in the earth from another dimension. The Hopis also told stories of giant, hairy creatures named "Saqua" that also came through the hole to steal sheep for food.

My reverie continued until Krista and Amber came in from school. Amber was crying. "Mom, we have Bigfoot at our house. Everybody says so."

Krista scoffed. "All the kids on the bus were telling Bigfoot stories. I didn't believe them, but Am got real scared."

I pulled Amber to my side. "Honey, even if there is Bigfoot around, there's no reason to be afraid. You remember I told you about the gorilla at the B&I? You wouldn't be afraid of him, would you?"

Amber shook her head. Autumn had come out of her room. I had to choose my words carefully. "Just because you don't understand something doesn't mean you have to be afraid of it. Bigfoot could be just another forest creature who is more afraid of you than you are of it." I thought back to my first day here.

Amber had stopped crying. She seemed to be considering what I'd said. She acted like she wanted to say something, then changed her mind and left the room.

That evening after dinner, inspired by the girls' uneasiness, I wrote a story titled, "My Secret Friend." It was the story of a Bigfoot and a little girl who roamed the woods together. I read it to the girls later.

When I went to bed, I fell instantly into a deep sleep.

Soon I stood in front of my dresser, looking into the mirror. At first, the surface appeared misted and pearled, like the inside of a shell. A deep, emerald green replaced this. A face that was not mine began to form and I stood staring at the elderly Native American man I had glimpsed before. As I looked into his eyes, I melted into the cold greenness of a world that was to become my classroom.

I stood beside the old man on the spot where our cabin should have been. The landscape had changed little and no buildings marred its perfection. Between the trees, I could make out the same stretch of ridge across the valley. I knew that the Carbon River flowed at its feet. I was the only alien presence in this Eden.

The old man spoke without words. His voice was a gentle breeze whispering through my mind. "I am the Dream Walker. All tribes know me, by different names, but I am One. I am your guide and teacher. Together we will walk past the campfires of a thousand nights."

I would have stood and stared but he began walking down a path that led to the river. I was compelled to follow. My footsteps were the only sounds in the stillness. I did not know it then, but the events to come had been etched in time like the letters of an epitaph carved in stone.

We reached the river as the first green light of dawn crept over the ridge. The path was draped with dew-covered spider webs. Like doilies studded with diamonds, they glistened with nature's perfect symmetry in the early light. The old man stopped where the trail curved to the right. His thoughts came to me again.

"I will call you by the name, Sallal. As time passes, you will understand why. It was once the name of a great healer in the village nearby. She also was a woman who walked in two worlds." Then the old man smiled. It would be one of the few times I would see him do so. "You have big feet, my friend. They make noise where there should be none. If we are to see what we have come to see, you must learn to walk like the creatures of the forest. Concentrate, and the way will come to you."

As his expression once again took on the sad, distant quality I had seen before, his thoughts came again, urging me to follow. This time I moved close behind him, feeling little contact with the ground. Our travel seemed nearly effortless but when we finally stopped, I was panting like a tired puppy. My breath came in shallow puffs that were visible in the early morning air. I realized that this form of travel would take some getting used to.

We had gone only a short distance when I smelled wood smoke. An Indian village came into view. Women tended campfires as the sun came over the ridge. Mist lingered in the canyon, blending with the blue of the smoke. I had stepped into another age.

The mist began to melt and the outlines of the village became clearer. A huge communal lodge built of red cedar sat in the center of a clearing. Individual dwellings, lean-tos of thick cedar bark, dotted the surrounding landscape. The women were engrossed in their morning chores, while children ran in play. A young brave checked his arrow tips in preparation for the hunt.

Near the edge of the forest, a small girl carrying a basket picked sallal berries. She stopped to gaze up at a tiny, brown sparrow perched on a tree limb. This everyday act endeared her to me for no other reason than she was alive and I was a ghost in her time.

Suddenly, a long mournful cry cut the still air and was repeated in the distance. "Skookum," the old man murmured in my mind. "Giants of the land."

"That's the most lonesome sound I've ever heard," I thought.

"It is not lonesome. It calls to its kind. Skookum have lived in the forest as long as the trees. Few have seen one, but they are often nearby. They do not harm us and we do not harm them. That is as it should be. Soon the north wind will fill the canyons, bringing snow and ice. Skookum will go to the great mountain where they rest until the Earth Maiden comes again, bringing leaves to the trees and salmon to the river."

He gestured in a sweeping motion toward the village. "Look well, and remember, Sallal. In the days to come, this village and others like it will be no more. The trees and animals will all but disappear. Pale men will people the valley, but Skookum will still walk the river. Nothing will change that.

"We will walk together again soon, Sallal, for I have much to show you, and you have much to learn. Tell no one of our journey. All this is for your eyes and ears alone. Think long on what you have seen."

I awoke standing in front of my dresser, then backed up and sat rubber-legged on the frame of the waterbed. A sudden rush of white noise filled my ears. John must be right: I *was* losing it. Fleeting visions of my journey skipped across my mind. I knew if I concentrated, it would come back in detail, but I wasn't sure I wanted that. I'd had dreams before that seemed real, but not like this. I could still feel the damp of the morning on my feet and smell the smoke from the village.

I needed some distance from what had happened to plant myself firmly in reality again. At that moment, I didn't feel I could trust my senses or my memory not to betray me. What if, by remembering, I thrust myself back into that world of the past? I couldn't take that chance without trying to gain some control over when and where it happened. When I gathered my nightgown around my legs to crawl back into bed, I noticed the dampness at the hem; Dampness that told me I *had* been walking in the forest. At least now my recent dreams made sense. I hadn't been alone and sleepwalking in the woods. I had been with Dream Walker. I just hadn't been able to perceive him consciously yet.

I lay awake, with my eyes open, pondering all that had happened until I heard the girls stirring. Like a zombie, I stumbled through the morning. John just scowled at me and left for work. When the older girls had left for school, I sat down to think.

I needed someone to talk to. John certainly wasn't a candidate. He scoffed at anything he considered supernatural. If I told him I'd spent the night in an Indian village hundreds of years in the past with a spirit guide named Dream Walker, he would have me committed. The fact that my nightgown had been wet would prove nothing.

My first impulse was to call Youdi, but even that was impossible. She had called earlier in the week to say she had to make an extended trip to Seattle to sell some property she owned there.

Then I remembered Dream Walker's words to me. "Tell no one of our journey, Sallal."

Even if I could talk to Youdi, did I want to? If I didn't heed the old man's words, I might never see him again. As confused as

I was by all that had happened, I found myself looking forward to Dream Walker's next visit. I had always been fascinated by mystical things. I wondered if my experience last night had anything to do with astral travel. Certainly some research on the subject wouldn't cause Dream Walker not to return. I called to Autumn to get dressed. I would try the local library.

The section I was directed to had listings on everything from UFOs to fortunetellers. After settling Autumn in the children's section, I began my search. I found several books on astral travel but only selected one. I didn't really believe it explained my nightly walks. Then I spied a whole shelf devoted to Bigfoot. I checked out several of these and some UFO books as well.

When we returned home, I fixed lunch and sat down with a Bigfoot book. My scalp prickled when I came upon a sketch that looked nothing like the illustrations I'd drawn for "My Secret Friend." I recalled the screams I'd heard and imagined this scary-looking fellow calling to his kind. At the end of the book, I found the same legend of Bigfoot coming through the dimensions that Youdi had told me about. I found no reference to the word *Skookum*.

The next book to catch my interest was a paperback on UFOs. It was an old Frank Edwards compilation of sightings from the 1950s. As I skimmed through the yellowed pages, the name Orting caught my eye. I read eagerly.

> At 7:44 P.M., April 1, 1959, came the first hint of tragedy — a radio emergency call from a C-118 plane with four men aboard, which had taken off from McCord Air Force Base, Tacoma, Washington, at 6:30 that

morning. "We've hit something — or something has hit us." A few seconds of chilling silence then the pilot yelled, "Mayday! Mayday!" — Distress in any language. And then the final message; "This is it! — This is it!"

The big transport tore itself to bits on the side of a mountain between Sumner and Orting. There were no survivors and the military quickly cordoned off the area to keep civilians away from the scene.

APRO representatives were able to locate numerous witnesses who had seen the plane in its final moments. The witnesses all described two orange or yellowish objects following close behind the C-118.

Other similar objects had been reported earlier in the evening from many points in the same general area. The McCord Air Force Base told the press that the glowing objects were only parachute flares, part of a project by nearby Fort Lewis. The Fort Lewis news chief said that no such activity was in progress that night.

Perhaps the most damning developments in this particular case are these:

1. Troops were quickly brought in from Fort Lewis to cordon off the area. Other military men interviewed residents near the crash scene and warned them not to talk about anything related to the crash.

2. The pilot had radioed that the plane had been hit by something...or had hit something. Part of the tail assembly had been torn off and was later found in the hills on the north side of Mt. Rainier, miles from the scene of the crash.

My heart was pounding by the time I finished reading. I couldn't wait to show this to Youdi. She had lived in this area her entire life and I wondered if she knew anything about it. From my seat at the kitchen table, I could see the top of the ridge through the trees. Somewhere on that very ridge, four men had died twenty years ago. I wondered just exactly what had caused their plane to crash. It was another mystery to explore.

Rain beat down as if someone were throwing stones against the windows. The girls startled me when they burst through the door. I hadn't realized it was so late. I went to check on Autumn and found her asleep with a book in her hand.

Toward evening, the rain stopped for a while and I took the opportunity to walk to the river and sit on a boulder. The western half of the sky was clear and blue, while the rest resembled a week-old bruise. It would soon rain again.

As I watched the sun set, the sky changed to a delicate rose with streaks of vibrant orange. A blue heron dove to pluck a fish from the water. This time it rose into the pinkness of the sky and diminished as it flew off into the distance.

Walking back to the cabin, I realized I was looking forward to going to sleep.

My dreams that night were my own. Dream Walker didn't come to take me with him into the past. I woke feeling disappointed.

When everyone had left for the day, I bundled Autumn up and we walked to the river. It was one of those days when the clouds hung so low they felt like a ceiling, but I just couldn't bring myself to stay inside. Robust conifers grew thick on every side of the trail but the bare bones of alder and maple gave the woods a sense of desolation that matched my mood. Gray clouds swirled as we stood on the levee road.

Autumn gave my hand a squeeze. "Are you sad, Mom?"

"No, honey, just thinking."

"Let's think of something happy. I know... let's go see Greg and Randy."

I smiled and we shifted direction at the end of Youdi's path and made our way back toward the cabins. When we reached the spot where I had been surprised by something on the first day, I shivered. I hadn't been on this path since. Although nothing remained of my experience but a small bit of hair in a leather pouch, this place would always hold memories for me.

Autumn tugged at my hand. "Come on, Mom."

When we reached the pile of huge, rotting logs behind Youdi's cabin, I once again had the sensation of entering a lost, enchanted world. No matter what the season, there was such beauty here. For an instant I seemed to see through the eyes of memory. *I had walked with a child like this in the past.* Then, just as quickly, I saw a glimpse of the future. In the muted light, I saw the woman my daughter would one day become. The scenes flashed through my mind like frozen pieces of time.

It dawned on me, suddenly and powerfully, that this valley had been waiting all this time. Our arrival was the spark that had set the fires burning again. I felt sure then that Dream Walker would return. I knew my journey with him had been more than a dream. I just had to be patient and have faith.

Chapter Six

Speak not — whisper not;
Here bloweth thyme and bergamot...

Breathe not — trespass not;
Of this green and darkling spot,
Latticed from the moon's beams,
Perchance a distant dreamer dreams;
Perchance upon its darkening air
The unseen ghosts of children fare.

— *Walter de la Mare*
"The Sunken Garden"

My spirits were greatly improved by the time I knocked on Emily's door. Greg let us in, then he and Autumn ran off to the boys' room to play. Emily was lying on the couch that faced the picture window in their living room. She looked ghastly. Her hair was lank and greasy and great purple circles ringed her doe-like eyes. I sat down beside her. "Are you okay?"

She sighed. "I'm really tired, Sal. I haven't slept much the last few nights. Greg has been waking up at all hours." She looked at me. "He claims there are monkeys outside his window. I insisted he was just having bad dreams but he refuses to sleep in his room anymore. He shares the bed with Curt and me out here now. He isn't exactly afraid... he just says they chatter all night and won't let him sleep. Randy doesn't seem to hear anything."

"Did Greg watch some spooky TV show that could have put these ideas in his head?"

"Not that I know of. But the funny thing is, sometimes I've heard what I thought was chattering and deep grunts when I've gone in to check on the kids. Your mind plays tricks on you when you're low on sleep, I guess. The other night I could have sworn I heard someone screaming outside, off in the distance. Whatever is going on, I wish it would stop. Curt's getting testy about sharing our bed. Greg is a restless sleeper and Curt has to get up real early to go to work."

Emily sat up with what seemed like great effort. "Can I come use your phone to call Mom? It might help if we could stay with her awhile."

We rounded up the kids and walked to our cabin. Youdi didn't answer her phone. After several tries, Emily gave up and took the boys home to take a nap.

When the bus came and went and there was no sign of Amber, I called Krista at a friend's house where she had stayed to play after school.

"Amber got off the bus when I did, Mom. She said she was going to walk over to Shannon's house across the river. I told her you'd be mad but she said she'd call home when she got there."

Shannon was a girl Amber had met at school. She was Amber's only friend and had been home sick for several days. I knew Amber missed her. Her family didn't live far, but Amber would have to walk along the busy highway, then cross the bridge to get there. Autumn and I piled into the car and sped down the road. My heart was pounding as I drove. Visions of logging trucks and kidnappers filled my head. When we came to the intersection where our road met the highway, Autumn called out, "Hey, Mom! Amber's over there!"

I looked to where she pointed and gasped. Amber's crumpled form lay in the weed-choked openings of one of the abandoned, brick coke ovens. I burst from the car calling her name, then gathered her sobbing body close. Horrible scenarios chased each other through my mind. "Am, honey, are you all right? What happened?" I was too glad to see her to be angry. Her sobs subsided into coughs.

"It was horrible, Mom. I was walking to Shannon's when this huge bird swooped down over my head. I thought it was going to pick me up and eat me. It was SO big. I think it was a pterodactyl.

Coke ovens

We've been learning about dinosaurs in school, and it looked just like one. It was blue, with a long neck.

"Please don't be mad. I just wanted to see Shannon. I promise I'll never get off the bus again without asking. I don't ever want to walk on the road again."

My terror turned to amusement on the drive home. I tried hard to keep a straight face. Amber had seen her first heron. I felt she had learned her lesson, so I didn't tell John about her adventure. I had no doubt he would punish her if he knew.

I glanced into the mirror on my way to bed that night and Dream Walker's face gazed back. I felt myself pass over into the dream world.

Gripping my old pink bathrobe around me like a favorite glove, I followed Dream Walker down the trail. In my world, it had been raining. Here, the stars were at their most brilliant. We paused a moment when we reached the openness of the valley to appreciate the night sky. A lovely thought came from his mind to mine. "My people believe that the stars are the campfires of the ancestors." I smiled as we continued on. I would never view the stars the same way again.

Whatever happened next, I was glad to be here with him. I didn't know if this was another reality, or a dream. I didn't care.

"What is reality?" His thought came to me.

It dawned on me that he was right. In the 1700s the "reality" of my day would have been considered black magic. Anyone expounding on theories such as TV or even modern medicine would have been burned at the stake!

Dream Walker and I moved silently through the forest. I had somehow learned to move as a shadow, leaving no trace of my passing. I was a spirit moving between two worlds. The air held a hint of frost and I knew winter wasn't far off here.

To our left, the river flowed over the same stones as it had for centuries, before any man walked here. Straight off the glaciers of Mt. Rainier, it wound its way to Puget Sound no matter who walked its banks.

We made our way along the mossy trail until the village came into view. In this world, it was morning now. The women and young girls were on their way into the woods carrying loosely woven baskets and pointed sticks. Dream Walker's thoughts came, "They go to gather the last harvest for the time when the land sleeps. They will spend many months inside by the fires."

We followed the women into the forest. I was amazed at some of the things they collected, although others were familiar from my treks with Youdi. "Your friend has taught you well, Sallal. She remembers much of the old ways you have forgotten."

I accepted what he said, though I didn't fully understand. I noticed, as the women worked, the creatures of the woods fed calmly nearby. They did not flee, as I would have expected, as the women moved from place to place, digging roots or picking leaves. Dream Walker nodded. "The animals know they have nothing to fear from these women. They are the gatherers, not the hunters. There would be no animals in sight if the braves were near."

One of the women stopped what she was doing and gestured to the others nearby. Soon all stood staring at a muddy patch of ground. Dream Walker explained, "Skookum has passed this way. The people sometimes find their giant tracks. They are larger than those of two brave's feet combined. Even though Skookum are all around us, they do not show evidence of their presence often. They can run faster than any deer and disappear like a wisp of smoke if they feel threatened. It is said a person who sees Skookum is changed forever.

"I once knew a woman who had been touched by Skookum. She was gathering one day and stopped by a long fall of water. In the pool beneath her was a giant brown creature, digging roots with a stick. She was so startled she lost her footing and fell to the pool below. Her head hit the rocks. When she awoke, she was being lifted from the water by the creature. He gazed into her eyes as he set her gently on the bank. Then, as she watched, the air shimmered, and he disappeared. He left behind only a horrible odor.

"When she stumbled into the village hours later, she had streaks in her hair as yellow as sunbeams. For the rest of her days she lived with the ancestors, even though she still lived in the forest. She became a great healer: the medicine woman, Sallal."

I looked to where the women were huddled in a small circle. It was then I noticed the one Dream Walker had spoken of... the woman with sunbeams in her hair.

I smelled coffee and discovered I was back in my bed. I stumbled into the kitchen, and sat at the table. John had a sneer when he spoke, "Well, if it isn't the midnight wanderer."

I froze. How could he know? Did I talk in my sleep? Or did my physical body actually come along on my journeys? It must, because my shoes and my robe had been wet. I chose my next words carefully.

"What do you mean? I just woke up."

"Sal, you sleep so soundly I sometimes wonder if you're even there."

I tried to hide my relief. The girls came wandering in and the conversation changed to more mundane things. Everyday things... Was there any such thing as everyday anymore? My nights and days were now divided between walking with spirits and a legend coming to life. My life revolved around a journey in the past and mysteries in the present. I had no doubt the strange events in my waking world had only just begun. What would come next, I couldn't even guess.

Autumn interrupted my thoughts, "Mom, did you know Greg has monkeys at his house? They come at night to look in his window and they whistle and talk to him so he can't go to sleep. I wish they'd come to our house. I like monkeys. If they were sad like the one at the B&I, I'd make them feel happy again."

I smiled and stroked her head, "Get dressed, honey. We'll go for a walk."

Frost crunched underfoot. Old Man Winter had flung his icy cloak over the land during the night. Delicate ice crystals clung to the sides of the small plastic pond we had put out for the pair of ducks a neighbor had given us. The sun shone weakly and the air had a bite. The weatherman predicted snow for later in the day. I believed him. Our walk was brief and we returned gratefully to the warmth of the cabin.

It began raining shortly after we were back inside. I sat at the kitchen table watching streaks of water chase each other down the glass. The phone rang, shattering the silence. It was Youdi, back from Seattle, full of news about her trip.

When I related the UFO story in the Frank Edwards book, she was amazed. She had never heard anything about it. She suggested we meet at the newspaper office in Orting the next day to search through the old files. Youdi said that people in the area had reported seeing the orange balls, described in the report of the plane crash, for many years. She had even seen one herself. It had followed her along the road when she left her cabin one night.

The next morning dawned crisp and sunny, but no snow. By the time Autumn and I drove into town, the rain was mixed with snow. I had Autumn so bundled up she could hardly bend.

Youdi was waiting in her car when we arrived. The newspaper office was located in an old, white two-story farmhouse on the outskirts of town. A bell tinkled when we entered. Behind a much-used wooden counter sat a skinny, red haired woman wearing a dingy stocking cap. Her bright green eyes and crooked smile made me feel welcome. She peered over the counter at Autumn.

"Hello there, Sunshine. I do believe that's the prettiest head of hair I've ever seen. Unusual color. Are those curls natural?" She said, looking at me.

I patted Autumn's mop of Shirley Temple ringlets. "Yeah, it's so curly I have trouble brushing it. When she was a newborn, her hair was silver."

The woman touched her own carroty locks. "I'm Jane Campbell. What can I do for you ladies?"

Youdi spoke up, "We'd like to look through your back issues; the year 1959, in particular. Would that be a problem?"

"Heck no, not for me. But it might be for you if you have any other plans today. When my husband and I bought the paper about ten years ago, the files were a disaster. It looked like a whirlwind had gone through there. They're in no better shape today. I've never had a reason, or the time, to put them in order. I swore to myself the day I laid eyes on them that if anyone ever wanted to research something it would be their job to put them to rights as they went. Seems only fair to me. Upstairs and to the right, ladies. There's a ladder and a crawl space to the attic where they're stored. I'll keep the youngster occupied while you're lookin'."

Youdi and I looked at each other and gulped, then climbed the stairs to the second floor. A rickety ladder leaned against the wall at the end of the hall. Above it, a square hole covered with a piece of plywood was cut into the ceiling. Youdi volunteered to go first. Attics were where bats lived. I hated bats. She scaled the ladder, pushed aside the board, and then disappeared into the hole over her head. I shivered. This was a lot to ask in the name of research. After a few minutes Youdi called down to me, "Come on up, Sal. I don't see any bats."

I swallowed hard, tucked my long hair under my hat, and climbed into the dark hole. The musty smell of years gone by filled my nostrils. In the dim light cast by one small, dirty window, I could see stacks of old cardboard boxes. Newspapers lay everywhere, like a whirlwind had come through, leaving them in its wake. I heard squeaking; then a mouse ran through the streak of light. I relaxed a little. I didn't mind mice. Youdi pulled a string hanging from the ceiling, and the small room was bathed with light.

"God Youdi, this will take a week, not a day."

I scanned the rafters for bats and felt more comfortable when I saw nothing hanging. Youdi grabbed up an empty box. "Let's start with the earliest editions and work our way up. It shouldn't take all that long with two of us."

For the most part the papers were in good condition, considering some of them dated back to the late 1800s. After about two hours we had worked our way up to the 1920s. I almost lost it when a head popped up through the hole in the floor.

Jane beamed at us. "How you doin', girls? Hey, by the looks of it, this isn't going to take near as long as I thought. I figured you two could use a cup of coffee and a sandwich. I already fed the little one. She's asleep on the couch."

Food and drinks were passed up through the hole. Youdi and I took a well-deserved break, then went to work again. By 2:30 we had the papers in order. As Youdi dropped the last edition into place, we looked at each other. She spoke first, "I was afraid of this. It's common in UFO cases."

"You can't be serious. You think the government took those missing editions?"

"Can you think of another explanation? The only ones missing out of almost 100 years are the months when the plane crashed and those shortly thereafter. The military was in the area warning everyone not to talk about what they had seen. I'm surprised the crash was even mentioned in that book you found. McCord Air Force Base is less than thirty miles from here, you know."

We stacked the boxes in silence and pulled the board back over the attic hole on our way down. Jane met us at the bottom of the stairs with Autumn in tow. "I hope you two found what you were after," she chuckled. "You look like the losers in a dirt fight."

Youdi and I grinned when we saw each other in daylight.

"Actually Jane," I said, "we found nothing. Your papers are in order, except part of the year of 1959 is missing."

"Well, that's crazy. Now, why would anyone take a bunch of dusty old newspaper files? Are you sure that's all that's missing?"

We both nodded.

"Just what were you girls lookin' for?"

We told Jane about the plane crash and the orange balls that had been following it. I watched her face turn pale and reached out to catch her before she fell. Youdi and I looked at each other. "Sit down, Jane," I said. "I, uh... noticed that the river is just a little ways back from your house. In all the reports we've heard, the people who claim to have seen these orange balls say they follow the river. Have you seen them?"

Her expression became agitated. "I've seen them, all right. I've tried to explain them away, but I've yet to come up with an answer as to what they can be. They terrify me. It's gotten to the point where I'm afraid to leave my house at night. Those things follow my car." She turned to look at both of us. "You can't tell anyone I told you any of this. If you do, I'll say you made it up. I have to live in this town. I don't want people thinking I'm batty."

Youdi put her hand on Jane's arm. "We won't say a word. A lot of people have seen the balls. I've seen one myself. My grandmother saw them when she was a girl. If it helps any, I've never heard of anyone being hurt by them."

I looked at my watch. We thanked Jane for helping us and for watching Autumn. She gave us a weak smile. "You might try the newspaper up in Buckley. They've been in print as long as we have."

Youdi and I agreed to meet the next morning for the trip to Buckley.

The girls were getting off the bus when Autumn and I arrived home. Amber asked if she could go to Shannon's to play after school the next day. I called her mom, Janet, and told her I would be going to Buckley with a friend in the morning so I could stop by to meet her on the way.

I lay awake long into the night mulling over what we had learned, and not learned, that day. At about 1:00 a.m. I went to the kitchen for a drink. A tiny flicker of light caught my eye, then there were more. The dancing lights in the trees were back.

I wrapped my robe close around me and crept out the back door into the frosty night. The clouds over the ridge parted momentarily and a huge moon bathed the landscape around the house in its silvery light. I walked to the edge of the deck and down the slippery steps to the ground. A short distance down the path I stopped, scanning the trees for the tiny lights. In the bright moonlight, I could see none. The rabbits made scratching noises as I passed their cages, but all else in the night was silent except for the ice crunching beneath my feet. It was then I knew I was being watched. My hair stood on end. The moon ducked behind a cloud and the night rushed in to surround me.

Off in the distance, a dog howled, a pitiful sound. One by one, the tiny lights became visible. They danced amongst the trees like the reflections off a mirrored ball in a dance hall. Then they began moving slowly toward the river. A *presence* seemed to go with them. I was alone, standing on the path, freezing. I stood there staring at nothing for several more minutes before I hurried to the warmth of the cabin and bed. I instantly fell asleep and, that night, my dreams were my own.

Youdi arrived early the next morning. She said she would be happy to stop at Janet's on our way. I pointed out their driveway directly after the bridge on the opposite side of the river. It was the only access to the ridge across the river from our cabins. There were no other roads or houses for miles beyond. We followed a long drive to the house.

Janet's husband, Pete, was home, too. Their son Timmy was Autumn's age and, after a brief introduction, the two of them ran off to play. Youdi and I were invited in for coffee. When we were seated at the kitchen table, Janet asked, "Do you have friends in Buckley?"

I explained about the plane crash and our plan to search the newspaper files.

"I remember hearing about that," Pete nodded. "It was on the ridge toward Sumner. It's just a couple of miles from here, right close to where the meteor went down."

Youdi and I looked at each other. "*Meteor?*"

"Yeah. It left a huge crater. That was back in the 1950s too. Nowadays we take the dirt bikes up there to ride. It's filled in quite a bit over the years but when I was a little guy, it was a pretty spooky place. You could see where all the trees had been scorched around the edge and the hole was really deep. If you like, I'll take you up there sometime next summer. It's a rough ride, even then. The road washes out each year.

"I know that plane crashed close by, but folks I've talked to would never show me exactly where, even after all these years. When the plane went down, people gathered from all over. Then the Air Force showed up and made everyone leave, but not before they threatened them about talking. They also confiscated any film that had been shot. I'll never forget what one guy said to me. Some officer told him if he valued his life, and his family's, he would forget he'd ever been there. Twenty years later he still won't talk about that day."

Youdi closed her eyes and nodded solemnly. Pete had work to do outside, so he left us women alone. When he was gone,

Janet spoke, "You know those orange balls you two were talking about? Shannon's bedroom window upstairs overlooks the river. She sees them from there. At first she was afraid of them, but she's seen them so often she's used to them now."

I wondered what else Shannon had seen.

Janet asked Autumn to stay and play with Timmy and Youdi and I continued on to Buckley. I hadn't been up this highway since our first day in the area. I wondered if anyone had rented the old schoolhouse John and I had seen at Hucklechuck.

The folks at the Buckley newspaper office were very helpful. Their files had been put on microfilm, so it took no time at all to discover that several months from 1959 were missing there as well. I checked a bit further into the year and found a small blurb someone had missed. It referred back to the previous articles on the crash, but didn't give any new information. At least it was evidence that the story had been covered in the paper. Youdi and I decided to look at the larger newspaper files in Tacoma as soon as we could.

It wasn't until that evening when I was in bed that I realized I hadn't told Youdi about the tiny lights and the presence I'd felt the previous night.

When I lay down in bed, I heard Dream Walker's voice in my mind. I arose and stood before the mirror. At first nothing but my own reflection stared back at me, then my braids turned to white and wrinkles appeared on my skin as his face replaced mine. Dream Walker looked into my eyes and I crossed the invisible divide into the past.

The forest was still, as if it had been waiting for me to appear. Before us, the path stretched away in the moonlight, seeming a thousand yards long. Wind whispered in the treetops and the shadows on the forest floor wavered like disturbed water.

I watched in horror as one of the braves from the village rose from the underbrush, aimed his arrow, and brought down a giant bull elk. I hadn't even seen the animal before the arrow found its mark. I was sickened by its death.

The kill was instant. I watched the life of the beautiful animal escape as steam from his nostrils. Then he lay still. I found myself wiping tears from my face.

"Do not be saddened, Sallal. It is the way of the forest. The people of the village must eat to survive. They kill only when necessary and waste nothing."

The rest of the tribe materialized like phantoms from the surrounding area. Men, women, and children fell silent as the shooter spoke, thanking the emuluk for giving its life so that others could live.

It seemed only minutes before the elk was skinned, butchered, and packed on the backs of the tribe to be transported back to the village. Only a wet patch remained where the elk had fallen.

I compared this to the hunting of my day and felt shame for my fellow man. I had seen the "great white hunters" driving by in their pick-ups and jeeps — loud, bawdy, good ol' boys with cases of beer and automatic rifles. Compassion was unheard of. Killing was sport. Likely as not, the only parts taken were the antlers and the tenderloin. The rest was left to rot.

Dream Walker nodded. "The so-called hunters of your day have no respect for anything. What do you think they would do to Skookum?"

Dream Walker's words left me shuddering when I awoke. Our journey that night had carried a powerful message.

Chapter Seven

For thou art with me here upon the banks
Of this fair river; thou, my dearest friend,
My dear, dear friend, and in thy voice I catch
The language of my former heart, and read
My former pleasures in the shooting lights
Of thy wild eyes.

— *William Wordsworth*
"Tintern Abbey"

The weatherman predicted snow for the second time this week. Last time he had been wrong, but looking at the thick fog that hung like cotton among the trees and the falling thermometer, I wondered if this time he might be right.

Huge icicles hung like stalactites from the eaves of the cabin. The duck pond was rimmed in crystal.

I sat at the kitchen table thinking of my latest journey with Dream Walker as I sewed a pair of slippers from the rabbit skins I had tanned. With the fur turned in, they would keep John's feet toasty all winter. Christmas would soon be upon us.

How could I ever explain to anyone the link that bound Dream Walker and me? After such a short time, I could barely recall life without him. It was if I had always known him. His teachings seemed like reminders of things I already knew, lurking deep in my subconscious, needing only a nudge from my teacher to bring them to the surface... much like the time spent with Youdi.

I looked at the frozen world outside. Suddenly, the walls around me seemed like a prison. There was just time for a short walk before everyone arrived home. "Put on your boots and mittens," I yelled to Autumn. "I'll race you to the river."

She came charging from her room and together we clumped down the slippery back stairs. The first flakes drifted to earth as we ran laughing down the path. By the time we reached the levee road, the canyon and the ridge beyond were all but invisible. We stood silent, alone in a world of white. The billowing bursts of steam coming from our heaving chests reminded me of the dying elk.

Laughing, Autumn bent to make a small snowball. I did the same, but froze when I saw an eerie orange glow threading its way through the whiteness. I grabbed Autumn's hand and we dove over icy boulders and snowy sand until we reached the water's edge. Staring through the soundless flakes, I spotted a faint glow moving out of sight upriver. A few seconds earlier and I felt sure we would have seen one of the orange balls.

We retraced our steps at a more leisurely pace. Soon our cabin came into view, warm and inviting as a picture on the front of a Christmas card.

I thought of my midnight journeys: These were the days the people of the village would be spending by the campfires in the cedar lodge. I hadn't seen Dream Walker recently, but I knew he'd never disappear without saying goodbye.

I was surprised to see Youdi later that day. She praised my work on the slippers, claiming she could not have done better herself. An odd smile crossed her broad face. "You are becoming an accomplished seamstress. Where did you find the bone for your needle?"

Puzzled, I looked at the tool in my hand. "I made it from a dried turkey bone. I didn't even think about using a metal one, I just made this. Why is that?"

Her grin broadened. "Some things one never forgets. You seem to have an uncanny knack for the old ways, my friend."

The snow stopped around dark and the rain returned. It melted the snow that was on the ground. By morning, the run-off from the mountains had turned the river into a raging torrent. It wasn't safe to walk anywhere near its angry waters.

The girls were disappointed that the snow was gone. They couldn't stay home from school. Autumn and I spent the day in town Christmas shopping. The rain grew steadily worse. The newscaster on the car radio announced flood warnings for several rivers in the state. Even though the Carbon wasn't on the list, I had an ominous feeling when we crossed the bridge and saw water licking at the pilings. John and I watched the news that evening, but there was still no warning for the Carbon River.

John was already asleep when I came to bed. It had been pouring all day. Great gray sheets obscured my view as I passed the living room window. I couldn't even see the path. Entering the bedroom, I stood in the muted glow of the nightlight staring at the drops chasing each other down the windowpane. I had the feeling I wasn't alone. When I turned, Dream Walker's face was looking at me from the mirror.

I found myself standing outside under the eaves of Youdi's cabin. I was looking at the beginning of her path through the dripping, gray-green boughs of a fir. I looked all around for Dream Walker, but he wasn't near. My heart thudded, and I felt abandoned. Then I heard his thoughts from a short distance off... "Follow the path and you will see what you have come to see."

On edge, but curious, I moved slowly forward between the huge rotting logs, wondering why Dream Walker had brought me to my own time and not to the past. I had never felt fear on our journeys before, but Dream Walker had always been by my side. I didn't like moving through the night on my own.

I had gone about halfway down Youdi's path toward the open woods when I heard heavy breathing. I was about to turn and bolt, but Dream Walker's thoughts came again. "Do you remember the first day you came again to these woods? You were frightened on this path then. Continue on... he will not hurt you, Sallal."

I rounded the butt of a log and stopped. An enormous, fur covered man blocked my way. I gasped for breath when round, green-tinted eyes met mine; human eyes that held the wisdom of the ages. The hair raised on my body. I felt faint. Then the air was filled with the overpowering stench of burning hair and garbage... and he was gone.

In his place stood Dream Walker.

"The day will come soon when even the man you call husband will change his mind about many things."

The next morning it was raining even harder. The wind came charging in great walls down the canyon. I looked in to see that Autumn was occupied in her room, then sneaked out the back door and ran through the dripping trees to Youdi's path. I had to see, in the light of day, the place Skookum had stood the night before.

A faint, rancid smell still lingered as I crept down the trail. The air was thick around me. Believing in a mythical being was one thing. Coming face to face with one, if only in a dream, was another.

I was almost to the spot where Skookum had stood when a branch cracked behind me. I screamed, but the wind hurled the sound back at me. I forced myself to turn slowly and pushed the rain soaked tendrils of hair from my face. Water trickled down my back. I willed my eyes to focus. A small voice said, "I followed you, Mom. What're you doin'?"

Tears of relief mixed with the rain in my eyes. I grabbed Autumn's hand and we ran for the shelter of home.

Over the next few days the rain never stopped. The river became so swollen it filled half the valley. Even the driveway was a swamp. I had to wade out to bring in firewood. I had never before realized what the term "cabin fever" meant. When weak rays of sun struggled through the clouds one afternoon, Autumn and I almost ran down the squishy path to the levee road to see what the river looked like. We stood atop the relative safety of the muddy road watching the boiling, brown water that filled the canyon. It almost took my breath to see the raging torrent the Carbon River had become. The rain began pounding down again, and we were soaked within seconds as we raced for home.

The weatherman predicted another violent storm for later that day. Flood watches were in effect for almost every river in the state, but the Carbon still hadn't been mentioned.

First the girls, then John came sloshing in the door. His expression was grim. "We'd better pack what's important and store it in the vehicles... just to be safe."

My stomach knotted. "Do you really think that's necessary? I don't want to frighten the girls. I've been listening to the radio all day and they haven't mentioned our river."

John grabbed my arm and pulled me aside. He had a wild look in his eyes I'd never seen before. "I don't want to scare you either, but on my way home the water was lapping at the underside of the bridge. If it comes up much higher, we'll be stuck here with no way out. This is serious. Now, go and do what I said."

Fear clutched at my heart. It was hard to believe the river had risen even more since Autumn and I had seen it earlier. John looked over his shoulder as he prepared to leave. "I'm going out to check the river. Have the girls pack what they need." And he was gone.

I started for the girl's rooms, but then I remembered Pete and Janet. Their house sat much lower than ours, beneath the level of the bridge. I dialed their number.

"Hi, Janet. This is Sal. Are you guys still okay over there? John just told me how far the river's come up."

Static crackled on the line and Janet's voice sounded far off. "So far, so good. The waters still about fifty feet from the front door. We moved everything we could upstairs, and the cars are all packed. We're leaving in a few..." The line went dead.

Trying not to panic, I grabbed some pillowcases and headed for the girls' rooms. I told them to pack only their most important things; then I went to pack myself. It's amazing what seems most valuable when you're forced to choose. This wasn't like putting things in storage. What I left behind might be gone forever. I had just finished stuffing the family photos into a shoebox when the lights went out.

Screams pierced the silence as darkness descended upon us like a bird of prey. I could hear the girls crying for me. "Hold on," I shouted. "I'll light the lamps." I fumbled in my pocket for a book of matches, and felt my way to the shelf where the kerosene lamps were stored. I lit two, and carried them to the girls. Circles of light beat back the shadows in the small area preceding me. Outside the wind howled and rain came down in biblical proportions.

I heard a commotion and ran to the living room. John burst through the front door. He bent over and held up a hand until he could catch his breath.

"I've been checking on the neighbors. Curt and Emily have gone to stay with her mom until the danger is past. Esther left a note on her door saying she'll be back in a few days. I packed the rabbits in smaller cages in the car and opened the chicken coop so the birds can escape. Do you want to leave, or should we stay and take our chances?"

I hesitated only a moment. “I’d rather stay here until we can’t. This is our home. We really don’t have anywhere else to go.”

I fixed a simple dinner on the woodstove. “Back to this again,” I thought. Then John left again to check on the river and I put the girls to bed with their clothes on in case we had to leave in hurry. I sat on the couch to wait for John. I thought I was still

Alward Ridge during the flood

awake, but someone was shaking me. “Sal, Sal... wake up. It’s almost dawn. The river has topped the levee. I need to go check on the Duncans. I forgot about them. Their house is closer to the river than anyone’s. If they’re still asleep they haven’t got a chance.”

I felt sick. John was right. The Duncans had only recently moved in. Their house was at the other end of their narrow piece of property, beneath the levee road. I wondered if it wasn’t already too late. I thought about Pete and Janet again, too, as John banged out the door.

When I looked outside, an eerie green glow had seeped through the clouds to separate land from sky. Panic seized me by the throat. I couldn’t sit any longer. I had to move; to see for myself what it looked like outside. We certainly weren’t in any more danger out there than we were here.

I woke the girls and told them to put on extra clothes. We ate a cold breakfast and climbed into the car. The rabbits made small, whimpering noises in the back. I felt like doing the same. All around us, debris left by the storm cluttered the ground. Fallen branches scraped the car as we crept by. The entrance to the Duncans’ driveway was nearly invisible in the dim light and fierce rain. I almost drove past, until it was outlined sharply by a lightning bolt somewhere nearby. I heard the loud crack of a tree falling, and the car was filled with screams... including mine.

I drove slowly through deep puddles and overhanging trees toward a clearing full of cars and trucks. People were running in every direction, throwing things into the vehicles. I spied John and another man carrying a couch to one of the trucks. When John saw us he dropped his end and came running over. “What the hell are you doing here?" he yelled. "Do you have any idea how dangerous it is?"

I hadn't, but his attitude angered me. I moved close to his ear. "I was afraid to stay in the house with the girls. It felt like we were sitting ducks. Are the Duncans okay?"

He calmed down a little. "The Duncans are fine, but I'm sure glad I came to check. When I got here, they were still asleep. I had to pound on the door to wake them up. Then all these people showed up, and everyone helped move their stuff out. I don't think they'll lose much, except the house." John paused, then seemed to come to a decision. "You wanted to see what was going on. Let's get the girls, and I'll show you all something you'll probably never see again."

Like a paperclip chain, we held hands and followed John up a small rise off to the side of the house. As far as I could see there was nothing but boiling water. The roar of the water made speech impossible. The rain had stopped for the moment, but the sky looked angry. Huge logs rumbled by, tossed about like matchsticks. As we watched, several old growth trees tangled together in a whorl of water, forming an enormous logjam. Still more logs became caught until a massive wall had formed. Just when I thought it could hold no more, the biggest log yet came swirling downstream. When it came up against the barricade it was forced upright, where it stood, a tall tree once more, before it crashed down, breaking the entire pile apart. The last thing I saw before we turned to go was the entire corner of a building. As it came hurtling by, I recognized a stained glass window I had seen only once before — in the old schoolhouse at Hucklechuck.

A shout came from the crowd standing by the Duncan house. The river had broken through the levee. John grabbed my hand, and we all raced to the car. A voice rose above the roar of the river. It was Mr. Duncan. "She's goin' in, boys. Take whatever you want before the river gets it."

Before I knew what was happening, John ran for the house carrying a hammer and a crowbar. He motioned to one of the other men and together they disappeared into the doomed house. Seconds later a large roll of carpet came flying out. Then another after that. Next, knotty pine boards whizzed through the opening. I could see water seeping around the edges of the foundation to form a lake by the front door.

Another roar went up from the crowd as an ominous creaking began. I watched in horror as the house buckled. Half of

During the flood

it broke loose and went swirling away.

"JOHN," I screamed. "GET OUT OF THERE!" He didn't respond.

Several pine cabinets were propelled into the yard, and a pile of doors followed. The remainder of the house began twisting slowly, turning to face the river. Water rushed underneath and carried it away just as John and the other man dove from a window. My heart threatened to break through my chest when the two halves of the house collided with the bridge pilings downriver and were reduced to a huge pile of kindling.

I ran to John's side and screamed in his face, "ARE YOU NUTS? YOU ALMOST GOT KILLED, YOU STUPID ASS!"

He looked at me and started laughing. He laughed so hard he fell to his knees. When he stood back up, he was crying. Great, gulping, sobs that were silent against the noise of the river. Then he leaned close so I could hear. "I've never been that scared. But I couldn't seem to stop. All those free building materials going down the river. I had no idea the house was floating until I felt it move under my feet. I'm sorry. Take the girls on home. I'll be there as soon as I get this stuff loaded up."

I didn't say another word. I did as he said.

When we reached the cabin, the power was still out so I made coffee on the woodstove and turned on the portable radio to listen for weather reports. The announcer was warning the residents along the Carbon River that it would crest at ten feet over flood stage sometime during the night. Tired and shaky, I sat down to await John's return.

Hours later, Autumn woke me saying everyone was hungry. It was dark outside. I lit the lamps, and cooked some dinner. There was no sign of John.

It had been many hours since we had left him at the Duncan place. I felt sick with worry. After what I'd seen him do earlier, I could imagine all sorts of disasters befalling him, but I couldn't go searching in the dark. I sat at the kitchen table wondering what I'd do if he never came home.

After about two hours the front door burst open and two bedraggled figures stumbled in. John, and Janet's husband, Pete, slumped into chairs and laid their heads on their arms. No one spoke. I hurried to bring coffee and towels.

"Where have you been?" I asked. "I was scared to death."

He raised his head and stared at me with vacant eyes. He seemed incapable of speech. Pete laid his hand on John's arm and spoke in a halting voice. "After we left... the, uh Duncans, we walked up... up river to see if the levee was holding. It's still there, but only behind your place and Youdi's. Every place else it's... gone, just gone. It was tough getting through... thigh high water in places. When we climbed up onto the levee road behind your place to look up river John nudged me and pointed to the bank across the canyon. This gigantic, hairy *thing* that looked like a man stood up from where he'd been crouching next to a root ball. When he saw us watching him, he turned and walked up the bank and into the trees on the ridge. Every few steps, he looked back to see if we were still there." Pete paused to wipe a towel over his face. "That thing must have been close to eight feet tall. We saw it clear as day. It was a Bigfoot."

"I've seen him over there, Mom," Amber said. "I waved, but he didn't wave back. He just walked away."

I didn't realize the girls had been listening until Amber spoke. John turned, and spoke sharply to them. "You kids go back to your rooms so we can talk."

"There's no need to shout at them. It's not their fault you've seen a figment of my imagination."

His face crumpled. Tears rolled down his dirty face and disappeared into his red beard. "I'm sorry. It's been one hell of a day. I'm not sure *what's* real anymore."

Pete stood. He looked haggard. "I've got to get back to Janet and the kids. She'll be worried. We have to row to the house in a boat now. We're camped upstairs until the water goes down. I'll be in touch tomorrow."

After Pete left, John walked toward the bedroom. He moved like an old man. The cornerstone had been removed from his wall of disbelief and the wall had fallen in on him. I suddenly remembered Dream Walker's words, *"Soon, even the man you call husband will change his mind about many things."*

Chapter Eight

While yet a boy I sought for ghosts, and sped
Through many a listening chamber, cave and
ruin,
And starlight wood, with fearful steps pursuing
Hopes of high talk with the departed dead.

— Percy Bysshe Shelly
"Hymn to Intellectual Beauty"

When I opened my eyes the morning after the flood, rain was still crying down the windows. As the day wore on, the sun pushed weakly through the clouds. Mist rose like a boiling cauldron as the valley began to dry.

The destruction caused by the water was awesome. I would never have believed what the river had become, had I not seen it. A vengeful tool of nature, it had wiped out everything in its path. Now I knew why there was a steep bank behind our cabin. The decaying logjam behind Youdi's must also be a remnant of floods past. It hadn't occurred to me that the levee was built out of necessity.

In the following days, the Army Corps of Engineers brought in countless loads of huge rocks, called riprap, to repair the levee.

Pete had been right. The only place the rocks hadn't been swept away was behind our property and Youdi's.

Behind us, across the desolate valley of debris, I could see the root wad where Pete and John had seen the Skookum. The river channel had completely changed course. It now ran directly beneath the ridge. After several days, I could walk to within 100 feet of the opposite bank.

I told Youdi about John and Pete's sighting as soon as the phones were working. She said I should question them as soon as possible to get details. Each time I attempted to ask John what he'd seen he shot me a dirty look and left the room. I didn't realize how deep his denial went until Christmas morning.

Early on, John was in a rare good humor. Then he opened the gift I had made him. When he saw the pair of handsome, fur-lined slippers, he went still. His eyes took on a hardness. He rose, and left the room. I found him standing and staring out the kitchen window.

"I take it you don't like your gift," I said.

"I don't like anything to do with that little Injun. I sure as hell don't want some slippers she made. All you two do is chatter on about some stupid mythical creature called Skookum. I just want our lives back. There is no such thing as Skookum. It's all in your imagination, and..."

Something inside me exploded.

"You *saw* it, John. What does it take for you to pull your head out? At least I have an open mind. And, as far as Youdi goes, calling her names is rude. She's my friend, and I've learned some really useful things from her. Have you bothered to notice that we don't go to the doctor anymore?"

John screwed up his face. "Uh, no, I hadn't thought about it. What's that got to do with her?"

"God, you can be so dense. All those herbs and things in the pantry are because of Youdi. She's taught me how to keep us well. If the kids get hurt, I fix it. Maybe you're really unhappy with *me*. Is it the way I cook, or keep house? Is that it?

"NO."

"Well, what exactly is your problem? Maybe you're jealous because I finally have a friend. Youdi is a hell of a better person than those beer-guzzling, good ol' boys you get drunk with after work. How would you like it if I told you I didn't want you to see them anymore?"

"I'll see anyone I want to," John said, puffing out his chest.

"Exactly, and so will I. Grow up. If you don't want to admit what you've seen with your own eyes, that's fine. But don't take your stubbornness out on me, or on Youdi. Oh, and John?"

"Yeah?"

"*I* made the slippers for you. Merry Christmas."

The rest of the day went better. John must have done some thinking. Later he came out wearing his slippers. From then on, he seemed to look at me and Youdi through different eyes. It was the first time I had ever stood up to his bullying.

Shortly after Christmas, Dream Walker came into my dreams again. His first thoughts tickled me.

"The man you call husband is one stubborn pasaiook. He saw Skookum with his own eyes, and still he does not believe."

Then, it dawned on me. "Why you wily old coyote. You set that whole thing up, didn't you?"

Dream Walker did his best to look innocent. "I do not have the power to tell Skookum what to do. Things happen as they are meant to. Let us be off now. There is a celebration in the village."

The path we took showed no signs of the recent flood. This didn't surprise me. It was another time, if not another place. High above us, the moon hung remote and thinly veiled by motionless clouds.

As we neared the village, the sounds of drums and chanting reached out to me on the wind. There was snow on the ground and the people were dressed warmly in beaded finery. Some of the women wore capes of woven cedar bark to ward off the cold.

Around a gigantic bonfire, men and women danced while drummers kept time. Other fires blazed nearby. Huge hunks of elk and venison smoked invitingly over some, while others had a framework of aromatic sticks upon which a whole salmon dripped juices that filled the air with a wonderful fragrance. Carved wooden bowls laden with wild potato, camas bulbs, and dried sallal berries were stacked against the walls of the cedar plank lodge. Dream Walker's thoughts came to me.

"The people celebrate the feast of the Spirits. It is time to give thanks for the bounty in their lives. Soon the lean months will be at an end. When the wind brings the cries of Skookum down from the great mountain, the people know the dark days are at an end. Warmth and plenty will come to the forest again."

A roar went up from the dancers when figures covered in brown fur ran through the village. Their high-pitched screams echoed long after they had disappeared into the forest.

When I opened my eyes in my own world, the screams still rang in my ears. For a moment I was suspended in time. Like a mild intoxicant, a sense of unreality persisted. It seemed each time I traveled with Dream Walker I had more trouble fitting back into my normal reality. Someone spoke my name, and the memories evaporated like a bubble.

I was watching the morning news when the name Hucklechuck caught my eye. The show was a special on the effects of the flood. It showed a ragged, 50-foot cliff where the Hucklechuck schoolhouse had once stood. The enormous maple where a little girl's treasure was stashed was gone, too. I felt sick to think we had considered living there.

As I put the bread on to rise, I pondered the chain of events that had occurred since we'd come here and wondered what the future would bring.

There had been no time in recent weeks for further research on the plane crash. We planned to look through the newspaper files in Tacoma, or even in Seattle when the weather was better.

Autumn and I walked over to visit Emily and the boys while the bread was rising. We hadn't seen them since before the flood. When Emily answered the door, she seemed surprised to see me. "What have you got, ESP?" She said. "I was just coming over to talk to you. I, um... don't know how to say this, but I've been seeing some really odd lights over the ridge at night. I was hoping you had seen them, too."

"What kind of lights, Emily? There's no way anyone can get up there, except through Pete and Janet's property. I don't think they'd let any hunters in to spotlight deer or anything. They're pretty private people."

"Oh no, these aren't on the ridge, they're in the sky. I haven't been sleeping well, and I get up in the middle of the night and sit by the big window here. For several nights in a row, about 2:00 a.m., there's a big, white light that hovers over the treetops. Sometimes it just stays in one place, but other times it moves slowly along the ridge, then back, until it finally disappears from sight.

"Last night it started moving away, then it stopped. Several much smaller lights, of all colors, came up from the trees and were absorbed into it. Then it moved on. I know it sounds silly, but I saw it. It's not the moon, I could see that, and it's too big to be a star. Are you sure you haven't seen anything?" Emily looked like she was begging me to believe her.

I hadn't been looking out our back window much lately. I'd been with Dream Walker during the middle of the night, but I couldn't tell Emily that. Maybe Youdi's researcher friend was on the right track. I knew it had taken a lot of courage for Emily to tell me about the lights she'd seen. I could tell my silence was making her uncomfortable. If I didn't say the right thing, she might never trust me again.

"I've been going to bed early since the flood. I can't seem to catch up on sleep. But I'll sit up on the couch tonight as long as I can to see if I can see anything across the river. Did you say about 2:00 a.m.?"

I could see a look of relief pass over Emily's face and she nodded before casting her eyes downward again. "Thanks, Sal. I was afraid you wouldn't believe me."

That night, I made myself comfortable on the couch facing the window that overlooked the ridge. I read one of the Bigfoot books from the library written by a researcher named John Green. Every so often, I turned out the lamp and scanned the night sky. There was just a crescent of moon.

Midnight came and I had seen nothing. At 2:00 a.m., I was ready for bed. I turned out the lamp and looked out, one last time. A small red light blinked in the sky above the ridge. Then I saw a huge, white light cruise into sight and stop above the red one. More red and blue lights rose from the trees to meet the white one, then disappeared within it. I counted five of each color. After a few minutes, the white light moved up river toward Mt. Rainier. I watched it until it went out of sight.

I sat back on the couch, stunned at what I'd just seen. I could hear Dream Walker's thoughts in my mind. "They are the campfires of the ancestors, Sallal. They will be visible more often in the days ahead when Skookum come down from the mountain."

Early the next morning I called Youdi. She said she would report the light show to her researcher friend, Paul, in California.

That night around bedtime, the rain came again. Lightning snaked over the dark, thickly timbered ridge. The valley was filling fast with mist and the clouds hung low — so low, no lights would be visible.

Dream Walker's face looked back at me as I passed my dresser on the way to bed.

It was morning in the other world. As our journey began, I inhaled the wood smoke of campfires past. This time we did not linger near the village but continued until we reached a high cliff overlooking the river. When I followed Dream Walker's gaze, I saw miles of ancient forest and, beyond this, at the edge of yesterday where no man had ever walked, the giant trees still stood. "Come, my friend. I will show you the sign of change. It is only visible when great things are about to happen."

We glided down a rock-strewn path to the valley floor. Once more, the feeling came that I was not a stranger to this valley. I was treading familiar ground. In forgotten, happy times, I had walked this trail before.

When we rounded a large boulder, Dream Walker stepped aside. The scene before me took my breath away. A pool the color of emeralds reflected the morning sun. Waist-high maidenhair ferns reached delicate fingers to the water below. At our feet grew a carpet of moss and wildflowers. Above, the boughs of fir and cedar formed a protective canopy that all but enclosed us in a wilderness cathedral. A massive gray boulder shaped like a beached whale formed the pool. The river slowed behind it, lapping peacefully at its great belly. I had never felt so close to heaven anywhere else.

"Look closely at the rock, Sallal."

I had been so stunned by the sheer beauty of the place I'd forgotten why we'd come. Toward the tail of the great beast, I noticed a large circle. Carved three to four inches deep on one side, slightly less on the other, it looked out of place in the wilderness landscape. In the center of the circle was an odd symbol that resembled an upside down capital F, except it had three horizontal lines instead of two. The diameter of the circle was about 2 1/2 feet.

Toward the head of the whale, about 6 feet from the large circle, was a smaller one. In it was a crude carving of the face of the being I had seen on Youdi's trail. My breathing became shallow.

The face in Whale Rock, 1991

"Who made these pictures, Dream Walker? And what does the symbol mean?"

"No one knows, my friend. They have appeared here before in times past. Then they disappear, always before a great change occurs in the valley. They are said to be a warning from the ancestors. Wise men heed this warning."

The shrill ringing of the phone yanked me from sleep. It was Youdi. "Get up, Sal. I'll be by to pick you up in an hour. We've got to get out to Burnett. I've always wondered where Skookum go during the winter. I may have found the answer." Before I could say a word, the line went dead.

I hurried to fix breakfast and scoot everyone out the door. I was zipping Autumn's coat when I heard Youdi's car pull in. She came bursting in the door, then we followed her back out. She handed me a newspaper clipping and off we went. I read as we drove up the mountain.

It didn't take long to reach the tiny town of Burnett. A clerk at the combination store and post office gave us directions to the farm mentioned in the article. We parked amongst a gathering of cars and trucks and hurried across a snow-covered field to where the crowd was milling about. I could hear some of the men muttering.

"The whole area's riddled with old mines. Oughta make that mining company fill 'em all in. You never know when the ground's gonna open up and swallow you."

I gripped Autumn's hand tightly as we edged closer to a huge hole in the ground. Nearby, someone picked up a rock and dropped it in one of the fissures radiating out from the sinkhole.

Everyone waited in silence, but we didn't hear the stone hitting bottom.

The yawning mouth of the cavern covered more area than my cabin and Youdi's combined. A wave of dizziness threatened to overwhelm me as I looked into its depths. I sat down in the wet snow before I fell. I could hear Youdi's voice coming from a long way off. "Sal...Sal... are you okay?"

"I'm all right. Looking down there made me think of something Esther told me. One of the mines up here by Burnett caved in once. When the owners discovered the victims were Chinese, they covered over the opening and walked away. She said for years there have been sightings of phantom trains and lines of men with picks and shovels. One woman wrecked her car trying to avoid the headlight of the train."

Youdi nodded solemnly. "Don't discount Esther's story. I have heard these tales myself. I had something else in mind when I looked into the hole. My people have always talked of tunnels and caves within the mountain. *Tahoma*, as Mt. Rainier was once called, is where Skookum have always been said to disappear during the winter months. The fact that there are so many mineshafts and abandoned tunnels quite near to us means that Skookum may hibernate closer than in the past. I'll tell Paul about these tunnels when I return home today.

"I have a feeling the existence of these tunnels may hold the answer to another strange phenomena in the area. For years, there have been claims of deep rumblings in the ground. Some have heard the sounds of heavy machinery in our valley. Smells of intense heat have also been mentioned. Since the mines shut down almost 100 years ago, there has been no industry of any kind within thirty miles of us. I've heard the sounds myself, but have no explanation for them. Paul may have heard of this happening elsewhere."

It began to snow as we wound our way back down the mountain. When we reached the valley, the flakes had turned to rain.

After Youdi left, I felt at loose ends. No matter what else I tried to concentrate on, my mind was consumed by the ongoing riddles surrounding me. I had so many questions but no answers. It was like trying to complete a puzzle with only half the pieces.

Although I still went through the motions of everyday life, usually completing my duties as wife and mother, I was obsessed with the otherworldly phenomenon that had become part of all our lives. It seemed the worlds of past and present, normal and mysterious were on a collision course. I had the feeling that sooner or later they would merge into one. Hopefully, then, we would have some answers. In the meantime, I would wait to hear what Paul had to say to Youdi.

Chapter Nine

Did I walk this way before
In some forgotten different plane?
Have I once lived and loved and died
And suffered ecstasy and pain?

— *Author unknown*

The next few weeks were uneventful. Even Dream Walker was conspicuous in his absence. I lived in a world of low hanging clouds and mist. The rain seemed endless. Youdi called almost daily to see if anything new had occurred and each time she sounded disappointed when I said no. It was as if the world was holding its breath.

Youdi arrived early on the morning of March 12 to celebrate my daughter, Krista's, birthday. The party wouldn't be until after dinner but Youdi planned to spend some time in the woods that day, something she hadn't done for over a month.

Krista's friend, Jennifer, was invited for dinner, so I began early to prepare the Mexican feast the birthday girl had requested. A couple of hours later there was a loud banging on the door. When I opened it, Youdi stood there, soaking wet.

"Come with me. I don't know how to explain what I've seen. You will have to see for yourself."

I turned off the stove, and slipped on my coat. Autumn was ready, standing at the door. The three of us tramped off into the dripping trees.

We walked further up river than I had ever been before, through unfamiliar terrain. In this area the trees were still old growth and the ground was almost devoid of brush. The air was damp with the ghost mists of early spring. Ancient whispers floated on the breeze. We rounded a boulder and the place was instantly familiar, though not in this world. The air fairly crackled with expectancy. I knew what I was about to see, but I hunched down and became a shadow among shadows as I waited for Youdi to speak.

"This has always been my favorite place to come when I want

Whale Rock, 2004

to be alone. I have visited this sacred spot for almost 50 years in every sêason. You and Autumn are the only people I have ever brought here.

"Never have I seen what I am showing you now, carved into

The symbol on Whale Rock

the belly of the great whale rock. I cannot help but believe this symbol, and the likeness of Skookum, are signs of things to come. Powerful energies have been released since your family moved to the valley. So far, we have witnessed only a small part of a great puzzle. Are you strong enough to deal with what is yet to come?"

I turned to face my friend. "I don't know where my strengths lie. That remains to be seen. All I can tell you is, I will do my best. I feel we have been brought together for a reason, too. I have been to this place and seen these carvings once before but only in my dreams."

Youdi's knowing smile spoke volumes. I had the distinct feeling my journeys with Dream Walker were no longer a secret, if they ever had been. There was a skip to Youdi's step on the way home.

That night when I saw Dream Walker's image, his thoughts told me the mirror was no longer necessary. I lay down on the bed and closed my eyes.

Instantly we were walking in early sunlight close to the village. Mist still ghosted through the forest, revealing trees and bushes then swallowing them again. A light frost coated the ground, but spring was beginning to show. Tiny buds formed auras of red and green around the bare skeletons that rose from the mist. It made my heart soar to see the village awaken after the long winter inside. Theirs was such a simple life; making use of what the Great Spirit provided and taking only what was needed from the land.

By the lodge, I could see my namesake, Sallal. She had grown older since I had seen her last, but there was no mistaking her. The yellow streaks in her hair sparkled in the light. She was with child. A great hump of life stretched her buckskin tunic. She turned in our direction, as if sensing our presence.

The breath caught in my throat as I noticed something I had not seen before. My hand went to the necklace at my throat. My dark green, oval pendant was an exact replica of the one the medicine woman wore close to her heart. But... how could that be?

"So, you have seen the stone at last. Both you and it have come full circle, my friend."

I felt as if a bright light had come on. No wonder this valley and the Indian ways had seemed so familiar. Now I understood why coming here was like coming home. I felt weak as I tried to absorb the implications.

I remembered thinking how odd it was, when I read through the Bigfoot books, that every place I had ever lived was listed as a place where sightings occurred. They ran quickly through my mind: Santa Ana, California, where I was born, The Skagit Valley, Maple Valley, and Bellingham in Washington, and the Priest River area of Idaho. My life to date had been a path leading me here. As Dream Walker had said, a full circle. But what about... "The pendant... My mother had given it to me. She bought it in Arizona when she was young."

I heard Dream Walker chuckle. "It is all connected. The necklace too has come full circle. In your life as Sallal, the medicine woman, it came to you from a pasaiook trader. He said someone made it in a tribe of stone carvers who lived in the dry lands to the Southeast. The stone was said to be Hyas Tamanous (highly magical) and to have great healing powers. You traded for it when you saw the stone had the shape and color of the leaves of the Sallal plant for which you were named. It was your proudest possession. You wore it always, close to your heart.

"When you passed over, the necklace should have gone into your burial canoe for the final journey, but it could not be found. It was not seen again until the day you came to this valley. Your necklace told me who you were, Sallal. You have been brought here once more for a reason. All will come clear in the days to come."

I found myself back in bed, clutching my pendant. I awoke slowly, as if rising through a thick, heavy fog. With the back of my hand, I wiped tears from my eyes. If I was here for a purpose, what was it? Dream Walker's words had urged me to be patient, but I was ready for some answers now. My whole life had changed since coming here and I wanted to know why.

I was still muttering to myself when I went in to fix breakfast. I turned on the burner to heat water for coffee, but it didn't work. I called to John. He tried it, but it still didn't come on. He went to find his ohmmeter to check the connections. When he tested it, everything read fine. He reassembled it and pronounced it fixed.

"Electricity is like math," John said, smugly. "There are givens in both that don't change. You women don't understand things like this. Watch."

He turned the dial to high. Nothing happened. John's face collapsed. "Uh... I'll just jiggle it a little." Again... nothing. He removed the burner again, checked the connections, and replaced it. Nothing.

"I don't get it. Use one of the other ones and I'll go check my manual."

I turned on each of the four burners. None worked. When I turned to tell John, I saw that the first burner I had turned on was glowing red, but the dial said it was off. I didn't question it; I put on a pan of water to heat. When the coffee was made, I tried to turn the heat off, but that wouldn't work either. Then I heard my washer filling in the next room. I was the only one who did wash. I ran to the new bathroom John had built.

Although the dial on the machine said off, the washer was filling. Smoke was billowing out from the back. I unplugged it and hurried to tell John. As I passed the stove, I noticed that all four burners were cherry-red. Then I heard the washer filling again, even though I had unplugged it. "JOHN," I yelled.

He came running.

Finally, by unplugging the stove and unhooking the washer from its water source, things calmed down. I was mopping up water and John was breathing hard. "What the hell is going on here?" He said. "I'm an electrician, for God's sake. These things can't happen."

We walked to the living room. When John flopped down in his chair, the floor lamp over his head went on. He ducked. “This is crazy.”

“Maybe something’s trying to get your attention in the only way you understand, John.”

It was the wrong thing to say.

“Don’t start with your supernatural crap. *That’s it.* You’re playing some kind of trick on me. You got someone to rig those appliances while I was at work yesterday, didn’t you? Well, it won’t work. I’m going to fix everything right now.”

I couldn’t convince him that I had nothing to do with the odd things that were happening. He spent all weekend trying to figure out how someone had fixed them to work wrong. After he had given up, I turned on a burner and it heated up. All the appliances were back to normal, until the next morning when we woke up to a flood in the bathroom and a stove that wouldn’t heat at all. John still blamed me.

“I hope you’re happy. I’ll be home from work early so we can find another washer and some new burners.” The floor lamp came on when he slammed out the door.

“Stupid, stubborn pasaiook,” I muttered, as I unplugged the lamp. “How could I be responsible? Women don’t know the first thing about electricity.”

Early that afternoon we loaded up Autumn and the three of us drove to the local appliance store and bought a used washer. The owner said he would send someone to deliver and install it the next day. At the junkyard on the outskirts of town, we found burners to fit my range.

John installed the burners when we arrived home; they worked great. Later I was in the bathroom when I heard Amber scream, "Mom, the stove's on fire!"

I ran to the kitchen, grabbed a flaming dishtowel from the top of the stove, and suffocated the fire. All the dials on the stove read off. John ran in and snarled at Amber. "You kids know better than to play with the stove. You could have burnt the house down."

Tears rolled down Amber's face. "I didn't turn anything on. I was in my room and I smelled smoke. Nobody was even in here when I came in." She ran crying from the room.

I turned to John. "How can you be so cruel? Take a look at the burners. They're all red, but the dials say off. Can't you get it through your head that something weird is going on? Quit blaming me and the kids."

Sali in the kitchen

When John slammed out the door, both the floor lamp and the ceiling fixture came on. I bent down and unplugged the stove. I decided in the future I'd only plug it in when I needed to use it.

The next morning after John and the girls had gone, a truck pulled into the drive. A young man unloaded my new washer. We talked while he hooked it up. He said he'd grown up in the area. When he saw my stack of Bigfoot and UFO books, our conversation turned interesting. He told me of several local people I might try to talk to about the meteor and the plane crash.

"Have you ever seen anything unusual yourself?" I asked.

"You mean like a Bigfoot or a UFO?"

I nodded.

"Well, I don't know if you'd call them UFOs. They aren't shaped like a saucer and they aren't all that big, but they sure are unidentified. My buddy and I have seen these orange balls in the sky along the river. They've followed us several times when we've been driving at night. He even took a shot at one once. That was something. He aimed out the car window and fired off his twenty-two. Those balls must have radar. The one he fired at took off, went straight up, then disappeared like a flash down the canyon. It was out of sight before we heard the shell whack into a tree behind where the ball had been hovering. We drove out of there so fast we left skid marks in the dirt.

"I can't say I've ever seen a Bigfoot, but I've sure heard those screams. I imagine everyone who lives around here has. Whether they'll admit to it or not is another thing."

My washer worked great. I thanked him and asked if I could bring a friend to talk to him about his experiences.

"I'd rather you didn't, Ma'am. My dad would be real upset if he knew I'd been talking to you about that stuff."

He hadn't been gone five minutes when I heard water gushing in the bathroom. I went and unhooked the new washer.

When John came home, he hooked up all the hoses again and plugged in the machine. It worked fine. The stove worked as well, but I unplugged it before I went to bed. About 3:00 a.m. I awoke to the sound of running water. Outside someone was speaking in what sounded like rapid Chinese. As I slipped out of bed, the ceiling fixture in the living room went on bright. I shook my husband. "John, John... wake up. I think someone is in the house."

He grumbled awake and walked into the living room. The sound of water stopped. The light flashed dim, then bright again. I could hear John talking. When he came back to bed the light was still on.

"That's the damnedest thing I've ever seen. I can't shut the light off. I wired that fixture myself not more than six months ago. I know it's done right." John had an odd look on his face when he turned to me. "You really didn't have anything to do with all this weird stuff, did you?"

"That's what I've been trying to tell you."

I saw fear in his eyes before he turned over to go back to sleep. I lay awake for a long time listening to the screams that echoed up and down the canyon.

Skookum were back.

In the morning the living room light had shut itself off. It was back on the lowest setting, where it should have been all along.

John checked the fixture and the wiring several more times before he left for work. Everything worked fine.

These electrical abnormalities continued, off and on, for about two weeks. Then everything returned to normal. One day, John tested the burners we had removed and the old washer that had burned up. All were in perfect working order. We spent all that money for nothing. John never did discover why things had malfunctioned and it bothered him.

The screams occurred almost nightly. At times I also heard birds chattering and high-pitched giggles. I asked Dream Walker if he knew what made them.

"Skookum are the mimics of the forest, Sallal. They are also shape-changers. When you see a deer, it may not be a deer at all. Skookum are part spirit and part reality."

That night in early spring, I accompanied Dream Walker on our longest journey yet.

Because of our mode of travel, I could now watch the miles of forest drift by without tiring. When we stopped, we were higher on the great mountain than I had ever been. The icy waters of the river sang to me as they tumbled over boulders in a deep ravine. Branches stirring in the breeze and the smells of earth and foliage rising between patches of snow were like the earth's music. I felt rather than heard small animals in the brush. Birds twittered their happy songs from tall trees. The forest sounds combined to form a symphony.

Dream Walker smiled. "You are one with the forest again." A crescendo of feeling swept over me. I knew what he had said was true.

Then all went silent.

From the brush beyond came the thudding of heavy feet. A huge, hairy hand swept back the huckleberry bushes across the river. In the dappled sunlight a massive, brown form squatted. He reached like quicksilver into the rushing water and plucked a three-foot salmon from the depths.

To the left of the creature a smaller, whitish form appeared. It walked to join the large one and together they examined the fish. Then they seemed to sense our presence.

A foul odor filled the pristine mountain air. It was a smell I was now familiar with. In the next instant both creatures were gone, vanished as if they had never been. The surrounding air shimmered with their passing. On the bank, the huge silver fish flopped until it slipped back into the cascading water, It would be dinner another day. I didn't realize I'd been holding my breath until a whoosh of air escaped my lips. Dream Walker's words came to me as we traveled back.

"Magnificent creatures, are they not?"

"But, there are young ones. I didn't expect that. I have never read of young ones in the books I have."

"Skookum guard their young carefully in high places such as this. The young do not come often to the valleys. That is why Skookum has survived until your day. Can you imagine what fun the pasaiook hunters would have with a young Skookum?"

Dream Walker's final words left me shuddering when I awoke. Then I remembered an isolated account I'd read of a young Bigfoot being captured by a railroad crew in British Columbia around the turn of the century. The men had put the creature they called Jacko in a cage and exhibited him. Eventually, Jacko had managed to escape.

I found the book and reread the account of Jacko. I felt better when I discovered that Jacko had not been recaptured.

In the same book was an account told to Theodore Roosevelt by a man named Bauman. I had seen this same story quoted in several books. I had been able to trace this report to its source, because I had the original four-volume set of books from my grandfather's library. The odd thing was, each time I came across this report it was quoted as coming from the wrong book. *The Wilderness Hunter*, the book the account was supposedly taken from, didn't contain anything remotely connected to Bigfoot. I finally found the account in another book in the set, and I almost missed it then. On the last few pages of *Hunting the Bison and Grizzly: The Wilderness Hunter, Part Two* was Bauman's terrifying story.

When I showed Youdi the set of books, she was thrilled. "These books are a rare treasure. I doubt there are many such sets in existence, especially in this condition. This is one of the few accounts of Skookum ever becoming violent. It makes me wonder what the two trappers did to provoke such behavior. After I first read this account, I had to believe these men were trespassing in a forbidden area, perhaps where Skookum raise their young."

I stared at Youdi. After my recent journey with Dream Walker, I had to agree. I thought back on what I'd read.

> 1907: Bauman and his partner determined to go to up into a particularly wild and lonely pass through which ran a small stream said to contain many beaver. The pass had an evil reputation because the year before a solitary hunter who had wandered into it was there slain, seemingly by a wild beast, the half-eaten remains being afterwards found by some mining prospectors who had passed his camp only the night before.

Bauman and his partner had, I believed, stumbled into the nursery area of Skookum. The account went on to tell how the men's camp and lean-to were destroyed several times (perhaps in warning) and their traps emptied. Throughout their stay, they found large human-like footprints and were followed and watched.

One night Bauman was awakened by something crashing through the bushes and a strong, wild beast odor. Then he caught sight of "the loom of a great body in the darkness." He fired his rifle, but missed. The thing rushed off into the forest.

After another such night, the men decided to leave the high valley, but they still had to gather their traps. Footprints of the beast surrounded their camp. During the previous night the beast had circled them, uttering a, "harsh, grating, long-drawn moan," but it didn't come near the huge fire they had built.

When they went into the forest together, they felt they were followed. Bauman volunteered to retrieve the last traps and headed off alone. When he returned to camp around sundown, no one answered his call. The forest was silent. The fire had gone out. All the gear was packed, but there was no sign of his partner.

Then he found the body of his friend. His neck had been snapped and four great fang marks were in the throat. “Footprints of the unknown beast-creature, printed deep in the soft soil, told the whole story.”

Bauman abandoned everything but his rifle and fled.

Chapter Ten

...and I have felt a presence
That disturbs me with the joy
Of elevated thoughts...

— William Wordsworth
"Tintern Abbey"

The next significant day was April 3rd, Amber's birthday. Youdi and I wondered if some monumental event would occur. We had no way of knowing this day would stay locked in our memories forever, like a first love.

During the previous night, I had slept fitfully, dreaming of Bauman's account. Several times I had been awakened by odd melodious noises coming from outside the bedroom window. Although I'd tried to wake John, he slept as though a spell had been cast on him. I wanted him to hear the strange singing sounds and what sounded like a flock of birds in the yard. I didn't know of any local species of bird that sang in the dark.

John had heard none of the screams or other night sounds so far. I hoped if he could hear them, perhaps he would believe. Try as I might, I couldn't wake him. Finally, I gave up and fell asleep.

When the alarm sounded, I awoke and began my day. After hustling everyone off to school and work, I made several dozen cookies for Amber's party at school that day. I was loading them in the car when I looked up to see Youdi and Emily standing a short way off. I could tell by their expressions something had happened during the night. They walked over to my car.

"Could we go inside?" Youdi asked. Her hands were shaking and she was as white as a pasaiook. Emily looked like someone in the throws of a religious experience. Wonder shone from her eyes. Youdi led her up the steps like a zombie. I realized Emily was in shock. I hurried them to chairs at the kitchen table.

"Sit down, you two. I'll make coffee."

While I was running water, Emily began babbling in an excited voice. Youdi held her trembling hands.

"You won't believe what happened last night. No, that's not so. I know you'll believe me; you did before about the lights. But this is like nothing I ever thought would happen to me."

Youdi interrupted. "Calm down, Emily. Just tell her what you told me."

"Oh yeah, sorry. Well, I got to bed really late last night because the baby kept waking up. It seemed like I had just dozed off when something, I don't even know if it was a noise or what, pulled me slowly from sleep. No, it must have been that awful smell.

"Anyway, when I looked out the window in the living room, there was this huge form standing by the tree out back. I gasped and pulled back so I could still see it, but it couldn't see me. It was watching something that was going on in the yard closer to the house.

"I turned to see what it was looking at. There were two smaller creatures, one gray or white, dancing around like they were playing tag or something. I remember thinking they were goofing around like Greg and Randy did in the sand at the river.

"I stood there frozen, watching these mythical creatures copy my boys. For some reason, I wasn't able to move. I've always thought all the Bigfoot stuff you and Mom talk about was interesting but I never really believed it. These creatures are REAL, Sal.

"The big one stood by that tree, with his hand resting on a limb, just observing the young ones at play. He never entered into the game. I kept thinking I should wake Curt, but I was afraid he'd be angry. He hates to be awakened when he has to get up so early for work.

"I'd watched the creatures for about fifteen minutes, when I knew someone else needed to see what was out there. I had to wake Curt. Normally I have to shake him and yell in his ear, he sleeps so soundly. All I did last night was touch him and he sat straight up. I whispered to him to look out the window and tell me what he saw.

"Curt gave me a puzzled look but did as I said. At first he didn't seem to see anything, but his eyes must have finally focused because I felt him stiffen, then gasp. He couldn't seem to move at first. Then he fell back on the bed and whispered, 'Did I just see what I think I saw?'

"When Curt sat up and looked outside again I realized he wasn't even looking in the right direction. I pointed to the yard, but the small ones weren't there anymore. Curt pointed over by the neighbor's fence and two big forms darted by. One stood erect and, as it moved, its shadow went across our kitchen. The other stopped and began picking at a small tree.

"Curt never did see the small ones... the two we watched together were big. The fence posts are six feet tall and they towered above them.

"Altogether, we sat hypnotized for close to three hours watching these creatures. It seemed like we both forgot that the other person was even here. Then we would realize how hard we were clinging to each other. I remember thinking I couldn't take anymore but it was like something was forcing me to watch. Curt didn't seem able to move either.

"We must have dozed off sitting up, but, just before dawn, we woke up and looked out the window again. The biggest one was crouched between two trees, behind a fallen branch. I pointed, but Curt didn't see it at first. When he did, he gasped.

"That creature looked right at me, Sal. When our eyes met, he nodded slowly... then he *disappeared.*

"Now that I can think back, I recall lights coming down the road. When this happened, the creatures bent at the waist and hid behind some bushes until the lights had gone by. Each time they did this, we smelled a fresh gust of that awful scent. Also, at times they seemed to just vanish, then reappear in the same spot as I watched."

Youdi and I looked at each other in disbelief when Emily paused to sip her cold coffee; disbelief, not at Emily's story, but at *Emily*. It was creepy. Another person had crawled into Emily's cast-off skin. Gone was the timid, mousy woman I knew. In her place sat a poised, confident woman. She was excited, but that was understandable. She had witnessed something from legend, right in her own backyard.

Emily's experience had changed her personality so drastically that I doubted anyone who knew her could doubt her story. What Emily had just told me took more than all the words she had spoken in the entire time I'd known her. The usually chatty Youdi hadn't uttered a word since she sat down. Her look told me that she, too, was stunned by the difference in her daughter.

Emily proved to be just as outgoing when we questioned her for details. There were a lot of them.

"What does Skookum look like?" Youdi asked in a hushed voice.

"Nothing like I would have expected. The biggest one had short, grizzled hair on his face, like a man with a couple of days' beard. But his eyes... Oh, his eyes were beautiful, but kind of scary at the same time. It was like looking deep into my own eyes in a mirror. He *knew* me and I found I couldn't look away. His eyes sort of glowed, like a cat's. They were completely round and convex. The actual eyes were behind a sort of lens that covered them. They glowed green in the semi-darkness. When I saw him again, closer, just before dawn, they appeared duller.

"When he looked at me and nodded, it was like he had acknowledged our meeting. I only felt afraid, really, after he was gone. But I can't even call it fear... maybe wonder is a better word. I remember feeling glad that I was inside. I can't imagine how I'd feel if I saw him outside in the dark; not that our window was any protection.

"It was kind of like watching a spooky movie at the theater. You pay money to see it because it's exciting. You know the monsters aren't real, so it's a safe kind of fear. I felt I was watching all this on a movie screen because the window framed it. It didn't seem real but I knew it was. I suppose on some level I should have been scared, but I knew they wouldn't hurt me."

Emily giggled. "Now I understand why Greg said there were monkeys outside. Although I don't recall hearing the chattering he described, or any noise at all for that matter, the young ones loped around like huge monkeys."

The Bigfoot Emily saw, drawn by Sali

"How big would you say the young ones were?" I asked. I remembered Dream Walker telling me Skookum seldom brought their young to the valleys. This was a rare sighting, indeed.

"I guess they were about half the size of the biggest one. I felt he was a male and the one picking at the tree was a female, but I really can't be sure.

"I just remembered something else that was odd. There was light surrounding them. Not the moon or the neighbor's yard light, it was too far away. They seemed to have light of their own; a sort of glow about them, or a light behind them. It's hard to explain. But their shapes were clearly visible in the night.

"If you will come over later, Sal, I'll show you where I saw them. We should be able to figure out about how tall they were by the surrounding trees. The head and shoulders of the big one were above the branch he was holding while he watched the young ones play. The other one, the female I think, was taller than the tree she was picking at.

"Could you bring John with you when you come? Curt asked to talk to him. He's home in bed, resting."

I didn't realize until Youdi and Emily left, but Autumn had been standing in the doorway listening. We hurried to the school for Amber's party. Luckily, we made it in time. We arrived home again about an hour before John was due from work. I had time to write down most of what Emily had told me. I figured if John read what Curt and Emily had seen he couldn't ignore his own sighting any longer. John and Curt had recently become friends.

When John arrived, I let him relax for a few minutes then handed him the paper I'd written. I let him finish without interruption. I watched as the blood drained slowly from his face.

When he was done reading, he set down the paper and stared into space. I waited several moments, but he said nothing.

"Well," I said.

"Well what? You don't expect me to believe this crap, do you?"

"Just because you won't admit something exists doesn't mean it doesn't. I've known people before who don't believe anything that hasn't been proven. 'Bigfoot *can't* exist because no one has shot one or found any bones.' These same people believe unquestioningly in God. I read a quote once that I've never forgotten: 'The best and most beautiful things in the world cannot be seen or touched, but are felt in the heart.' The quote came from Helen Keller. Just because she couldn't see or hear the rest of the world, do you think she gave up believing it existed? You've seen Bigfoot yourself, but you refuse to even talk about what you saw. Your friend, Curt, needs your help in dealing with what he saw last night. He's really shaken up. You're the only person he feels comfortable talking to because you've both had the same experience. Are you going to let him down? If you still don't believe in Bigfoot after you've talked to him, so what? You can still pretend Youdi and I are a couple of crazy women... we'll just have added one man to the group."

When I said the word crazy, a light went on. That's why John stubbornly refused to talk about what he'd seen. "Curt and Emily aren't crazy, John, and neither are you. Do you think if you talk about what you saw people will think you're..."

"OKAY, I'll go. Just shut up. Let's do it."

John grabbed Autumn's hand and we marched down the path between the cabins. Emily met us at the door. Curt was lying on the couch. There were deep, purple smudges under his eyes and he moved like an old man when he rose. He hardly resembled the dark, hefty man I was used to seeing. "Come on in, guys. I guess Emily told you what happened last night."

John and I looked at each other and nodded.

Emily had disappeared. She came back and handed Curt a steaming cup of tea. "You guys want anything?" We shook our heads. "I'll be right back after I take Autumn in to play with the boys." On her way past the couch, Emily bent to drape a sweater over Curt's slumped, burly shoulders.

The contrast between their emotional states was almost comical. Emily whizzed around pampering Curt, while he acted like a truck had hit him. I saw John watching them, too. Emily returned. "I'll take Sal and John outside while you drink your tea, Curt. Then when we come back, you and John can talk." Curt nodded weakly, but said nothing. We passed the big window on our way out of the living room and Emily paused to allow us to see the view of the yard. She was right; it resembled a large TV screen.

Once outside we examined the small tree where the shorter of the two adult Skookum had been picking things off. The grass in the area was smashed, but there were no prints. The tree was a cherry, about six feet tall. Most of the tender new shoots had been broken off. We found what was left of them on the ground below, their bark stripped. All the flowers were gone as well.

The tall grass was also smashed where the young Skookum had played. Again, there were no prints, only areas of ripped sod. On our way to the back of the house and the tree where the big Skookum had stood, Emily realized the tree was much larger than she had thought. “Oh,” she said. “I didn’t see him break off that branch.”

We looked up to see a ragged nub about three inches thick, and a foot long protruding from the trunk of an alder. The grass beneath was smashed, but no prints were visible. John stood under the tree, trying to reenact what Emily had told us the Bigfoot had done. I watched his expression change when he realized what he was attempting was impossible. His voice came out small and squeaky. “Didn’t you say that thing’s head and shoulders were above the branch?”

“That’s right,” Emily said. “He was leaning on the branch.”

I saw John gulp as he reached up. Even with his arm fully extended, the remaining piece of branch was out of his reach by about a foot. He looked green. Emily left and came back with a stepladder. John climbed until she said he was in the correct position. His head and shoulders were now above the ragged piece of branch. He was also standing on the fourth step. When John came down, he stood staring at the tree.

Emily and I searched the surrounding area for the broken off branch but it was nowhere to be found. I nudged John, and he came to life. We all went back inside.

Curt was still sitting exactly as we had left him. His eyes were shut and he jerked back when we came in the door. Emily rushed over to calm him. “Could I talk to you alone, John?” Curt said.

Emily and I wandered into the kitchen. I could hear Curt’s voice muffled by distance. Emily shook her head sadly. “Poor Curt. Until last night, he was the world’s biggest skeptic. Seeing what we did has changed him. All his fire is gone.”

"It seems to have been transferred to you," I said. "Do you realize what a different person you are today?"

Her face took on a quizzical expression. "I guess I am, aren't I? I feel honored and powerful; as if I've been chosen for something special."

I smiled. "You have. Only a few people have seen what you two did. Maybe Curt will recognize that and his attitude will change. While the guys are talking, I'd like you to tell me again exactly what the big Skookum looked like. Together, I think we can make a pretty accurate sketch while his image is still fresh in your memory."

"I'll be glad to. I'll never forget him, though. I'm not sure if I ever want to see him again but I'm glad I did once. As for Curt, I don't think he could take another night like last night."

While Emily spoke, I sketched. I erased and redrew the features many times, until finally she sat back with a satisfied smile. "That's him. That's Biggie. You've captured his likeness. Will you make me a copy of your drawing to keep?"

"Sure, I'll make you one next time I go to town."

We left for home shortly after. I watched a rainbow of emotions cross John's face, but he was silent until we had passed Youdi's cabin. I could see he was fighting whatever he had heard from Curt. Finally, I asked what he was thinking.

"Curt's acting weird; all spaced out and wimpy. Maybe he just wants attention."

"Is that what you were doing the night of the flood?" I asked. "You acted the same way after you and Pete saw the Skookum by the river. Oh, I forgot. You didn't see anything, did you? Maybe you've told yourself you saw nothing because you don't want to have seen anything."

John clenched his jaw. "That's not true. I don't think people see something like that just because they want to. If people who want to see Bigfoot see them, then why haven't you?"

I avoided the question because the answer would confuse the issue. Instead, I simply shrugged. "Didn't you notice the change in Emily?"

"Well, yeah. She is different. But who's to say that has anything to do with what they saw?"

I laughed. "What do you suppose caused such a change then? Both of them changed so drastically since yesterday even *you* have noticed. It's like Emily was reborn last night." John didn't argue.

Youdi had gone home but she called later that night to wish Amber a happy birthday. She said she'd been trying to reach her friend, Paul, in California, all day. Failing to do so, she had contacted another Bigfoot researcher in Seattle. He had a hotline for people to call if they'd had a sighting. He claimed all calls would be treated with respect and kept confidential.

I had a bad feeling about Youdi's call but she said Curt and Emily's experience was so unusual she felt she should report it to someone.

A man named James had called her back less than an hour later. Youdi said she would be bringing him out in the morning.

That night Dream Walker came again.

In his world, my old world, it was morning. The trees were mantled with the pale, misty green of new foliage. A cloud of small, buzzing insects obscured the path ahead. Our passing made no difference in the pattern of their flight. We were ghostly beings in this time.

The smell of smoke reached my nostrils. It mingled with another, more unpleasant odor I could not identify. I pinched my nostrils against the sweet, sickly smell. Dream Walker's words came to me.

"This will not be a pleasant journey, but it is necessary if you are to understand. Try to remember that all you see is in the past. You can only make a difference in your own time."

My stomach clenched when I realized what the odor was. It was Death.

My knees threatened to buckle when I saw what was left of the village. Bodies lay everywhere, some barely visible among the ashes of their dwellings. The longhouse was still smoldering. The smell of burning cedar mixed with that of seared flesh. From tall posts hung the still dripping, bloody heads of the braves who had fought back. Flies covered these cruel trophies like black sequins.

Women and children lay where they had fallen on the trail. They had been gunned down while trying to escape into the forest. Their lifeless bodies were grim testimony to the suddenness of the attack.

My heart ached when I recognized the body of the young girl I had seen talking to the sparrow. Her beautiful face was covered with mud, eyes open in frozen surprise.

Dream Walker said nothing as I stumbled down the path behind him. There was nothing to say. The grotesque scene spoke for itself. I knew who had done this.

I awoke drenched in tears and glared with hatred at the man sleeping beside me. He was a descendant of the animals who had murdered the people of the village. I didn't know how I could live with John or bear to be around any white man after what I'd seen.

Chapter Eleven

Like one, that on a lonesome road
Doth walk in fear and dread,
And having once turned round walks on,
And turns no more his head;
Because he knows, a frightful fiend
Doth close behind him tread.

— Samuel Taylor Coleridge
"The Rime of the Ancient Mariner"

Later that day, I peered out the curtain and saw a van pull into our driveway. Youdi's car followed. A pudgy man in green shorts and a pith helmet emerged from the van. Since last night's journey with Dream Walker, I had to remind myself to be civil to my own husband. I was in no mood to meet this white stranger.

Youdi knocked loudly on the door. When I opened it, the vibes emanating from the man on the porch caused me to recoil with distaste. Dream Walker would have referred to him as *cultus mamook* — bad work. I was surprised Youdi had brought him here. She kept looking at me like she had caught a skunk by the tail and didn't know how to let loose.

"Sal, this is James. He searches for Skookum."

James gave a grunt in my direction and then began justifying his presence on my porch. "I'm glad your friend called me. It pays to have a professional on the scene. Paul and I have been friends for a long time. I follow up on all the sightings he can't get to. It's always better to interview the people involved right away. That way we hope to catch… er, gather material, such as hair samples or footprints before they're gone." He turned to Youdi. "Could we go talk to your daughter and her husband now?"

James kept glancing at me under the rim of his helmet as he and Youdi walked away. He had shifty eyes. Our dislike had been instant and mutual.

John arrived home shortly thereafter. We walked over to see how Emily and Curt were handling the "great white hunter." John appeared anxious to meet with a professional researcher and hear what he had to say. Judging by his more accepting attitude, I could tell John had been doing some serious thinking about Emily and Curt's experience and, hopefully, his own.

Even though I knew John wasn't responsible for the carnage in a village I had seen only in dreams, I cringed and drew back when he grabbed my arm to steady me on the path.

A lively discussion could be heard as we approached Curt and Emily's cabin. When John knocked, the silence was instant. Emily scurried to get two more wine glasses and we sat on the couch. It was clear James had put himself in charge.

"Welcome folks, welcome. I was just telling everyone some of my experiences while hunt… uh, researching Bigfoot. The Big Guys are a cagey lot. I've gone to great trouble, in some cases, to lure them to me. Unlike some other researchers, I don't believe

Bigfoot is connected to UFOs, time warps, or any of that garbage. They're just animals. Sooner or later, someone is going to have to prove to science that Bigfoot exists. With the help of you folks, I may have that chance sooner than I expected."

We all looked at each other, but Youdi spoke up. "I didn't call you so you could catch a Skookum. I thought you were after knowledge."

"Of course, of course, that's my ultimate goal. But first we have to have one to study. No one is giving out grant money without proof."

"Why?" I asked. "Why not let them be and study them where they have always lived, in the forest? They've been here for hundreds of years. Why does anyone have to prove they exist at all?"

"To protect them." James glared at me from under his hat as he spoke. "In order to do that I have to catch one, only one. Then I can apply for a grant to study and protect them."

Curt snorted. "Whoever brings in a Bigfoot, dead or alive, will be instantly famous. That wouldn't have anything to do with your plan, would it?"

"Certainly not," James said, acting outraged. He stood, hastily tipped his helmet and stomped to the door, then turned with his hand resting on the knob. "If you people weren't going to cooperate, why did you call me? Never mind, don't answer that. You think about what I've said. When I return we'll talk more. Just remember, if you want Bigfoot protected someone has to prove they exist."

There was silence for several minutes after James left.

When I looked at Youdi, tears were rolling down her face. "What a horrible man. I made a big mistake calling that *pasaiook*. He's so pushy and arrogant. When we talked on the phone he sounded kind and sincere. I hope we're not stuck with him. I'll try to call Paul again tomorrow. He'll know what to do."

I had barely put my head on the pillow that night when I heard Dream Walker's voice in my mind.

"Things are moving fast now, Sallal."

As I followed Dream Walker, I could feel that his mind, like that of most elderly men, was somewhere beyond the path we walked. He must have heard my thoughts, for he turned and smiled sadly at me before traveling on.

The leaves of the deciduous trees around us had taken on their last burst of brilliant color before fading and dying for the winter. Even though it was spring in my time, in this world autumn was upon the land. These days would find Skookum traveling closer to the great mountain. Fall brought with it the timeless urge to walk the trail they had used for centuries past. Skookum could not ignore this urge.

These were the days in my own time when Youdi and I walked the woods gathering the remedy herbs. Ahead in the forest, I saw a bedraggled woman bending to pick some leaves. When she stood, I was surprised to see it was the medicine woman, Sallal. The green pendant hung from her neck. So, she had escaped the horror in the village. Cautiously, other survivors straggled out from the surrounding trees. A gunshot rang out and they melted into the forest like the wind.

A scream rang down the canyon, echoing off the cliffs. Then one dog barked, and then another. It was the high-pitched, frantic barking of pursuit.

Standing high on the ridge across the canyon stood a shape I recognized — Skookum.

The woods were permeated with a strange uneasiness. Life and death felt close at hand. As the forest watched, we stood silent for a moment, then followed a faint trail that led under the roots of great trees to the river below. I could see a line of shapes in the distance. They were traveling upriver, but they were so far off I couldn't tell if they were Skookum or the surviving Indians.

"There will be trouble. The pasaiook have built their boxes close to the ancient trail. These men have seen the footprints of Skookum in the mud and they are afraid. They do not know these gentle giants hurt no one. But, that too may change."

As Dream Walker's thoughts ended, I noticed movement in the trees. One of the great creatures lay listening on the forest floor. It appeared he was injured and had taken refuge beneath the tree. A low swirling mist helped to hide him. The Skookum cocked his great head, as if to filter out the noises of the forest. I wondered why he didn't disappear.

Just then, I heard the barking of the men's dogs. They had smelled the blood of Skookum.

When the giant heard the barking his expression changed to one of hatred. The dogs crashed through the underbrush, snarling and whining, the frenzy of the hunt replacing their fear. They were almost in sight when the Skookum forced himself upright. Hate mixed with agony, as he became a towering wraith in the swirling mist. Blood dripped from gaping gashes in his matted coat, as he placed his huge feet squarely, preparing to meet his attackers.

The dogs struck like a swarm of angry bees, biting his legs and propelling themselves upward to rip at his massive chest. Shrieks echoed through the forest as, one by one, the great creature ripped the savage animals from his body and broke them in half.

The sounds soon died as the lucky dogs slunk back into the safety of the trees. Dog corpses littered the forest floor. I gagged at the smell. The Skookum limped off into the mist as shouts and gunfire came closer. As a group of armed men rushed into the clearing, I heard Dream Walker:

"Soon there will come a day when Skookum will not win. The pasaiooks have weapons Skookum knows nothing about. There are so many of these pale men; they are like ants. You have seen what happens when Skookum are injured and their ability to vanish fails. If something is not done, they will be erased from the earth."

Our return journey took us along the river. Gone were most of the great sentinel trees that had lined its banks.

Gone also was the peaceful village and its people, except those who lived as wanderers in the forest.

Where the village had once stood, ugly box-like dwellings lined the bank. The brutal rape of saws and fire scarred the surrounding land. Like locusts, the pasaiooks had descended upon the valley. A mouth harp played a fittingly mournful tune as I journeyed back across the years to my own time.

I was writing a letter to my parents the next morning when there was a loud knock on the door. Esther was standing on my porch in a subdued pink and orange outfit. Blackjack was with her. When he smelled me he lunged in every direction, barking wildly, then pooped on my porch. "Sorry about that, Sue," Esther said. She yanked Blackjack's leash until I thought his eyes would pop out. Finally, he sat down, gagging. "I came to see if you had a visit from that idiot in the safari hat. The jerk damn near talked my ear off. He wanted to know if he could camp on my property to look for Bigfoot."

"What did you tell him, Esther?"

"Why, I told him I moved out here to get away from fools like him. Ain't no way I'm gonna let him park his bwana butt on my place. I talked to some other folks and he's been to their places, too. Mrs. Taylor sicced her dogs on to him 'cause he wouldn't take 'no' for an answer. Good thing she didn't tell him 'bout her husband's ducks. He never woulda left."

My ears perked up. "What happened to his ducks?"

"Well, the Taylor's heard them screams real close one night, a couple a years back. Mr. Taylor was worried 'bout his prize winning Muscovy ducks, but he was too afraid to go out and check. Next mornin', him and the missus found the whole bunch, 'bout forty of them, was dead. Somethin' had wrung their necks and stacked them like cordwood. Some a them ducks had teeth marks in their necks, but none was ate. Mr. Taylor ain't raised nothin' since. Says there's no point."

A few minutes later Esther left, after stepping in Blackjack's pile. She trailed it down the front steps. I cleaned up the mess, then went to call Janet to warn her that James might be paying them a visit. Janet assured me that James wouldn't be welcome there either.

I called to Autumn to put on her coat so we could go to Emily's. She came running in. I opened the door to leave and was startled to find Emily standing there. She hadn't even knocked yet. Her eyes were bright with eagerness. "Can I talk to you?"

I backed up. "Sure. Come on in. We were just coming to see you."

"I'd rather talk here, if you don't mind."

I told Autumn to take off her coat and go play in her room for a while. Emily and I sat at the kitchen table. She seemed ready to burst.

"Biggy came back last night, after that James guy left. There were no others with him. At least I didn't see any. He didn't stay long. He was out back by the tree checking out the ladder. I forgot to put it away after John climbed up. I watched Biggy for several minutes before he disappeared into the trees. His own light surrounded him. This time I paid attention. The light didn't come from elsewhere; it seemed to come from the Skookum himself.

"I didn't wake Curt this time. I don't think he can take anything else right now. All this has been a real strain on him for some reason. It's like everything he thought was real isn't anymore.

"Now I know what woke me the first time, too. Somehow Skookum have this ability to signal me when they are near. Biggy did it again last night, but this time I wasn't asleep. I knew he was out there. And when I looked, there he was."

I smiled. "That's neat. Your mom will be interested to hear that. She called to say she'd be out later today. She's bringing some CB equipment to hook up between my house and yours. Your brother, Mic, loaned it to her. That way you'll be able to contact us when something is happening. Maybe Curt will feel better if you guys aren't alone."

"That's great! Curt's so nervous he flinches at every noise."

Youdi drove in as we were talking. "You have that look again, Emily," she said. "They came back, didn't they?"

"The big one did. Did you bring the CB stuff?"

"Yes. Let's sit down, and you can tell me about last night."

Emily repeated what she had just told me. Youdi was quiet when Emily had finished. She seemed stunned by what she had heard. Then I realized Youdi had been gathering her thoughts so she could reassure her daughter. "Things are happening fast, aren't they?"

"Yes, Mom. Curt's scared to death. Do you have any idea why these things are happening to us?"

"No, but I believe it's all happening for a reason. If we keep our minds open and try not to be afraid, the answers will come. Just remember, even though all kinds of odd things are occurring no harm has come to anyone. Only good has come of this. Look at the change in you."

"You're right, thanks. I wish Curt could find something, too."

"So do I, Emily. Mic told me a strange thing that happened to him a few days ago. He was driving home from work, about dusk, when this long, flat, gray object came toward him in the opposite lane. He said it was shaped like a ramp, only bent. He was so stunned he slammed on his brakes, then just sat in the middle of the road as he watched in his rearview mirror. It zoomed out of sight behind him. Luckily, there were no other cars coming."

I suddenly remembered why I had been on my way to talk to Emily. "Not to change the subject, but I want to tell you guys about Esther's visit before I forget again. She came by earlier to tell me James has been going house to house around the area trying to bully someone into letting him camp on their property. Esther called him several choice names, including "Bwana." I'd say it suits him, you know, like the great white hunters in old movies. I think we're going to have trouble getting rid of that guy, Youdi."

"I think you're right. I'm so sorry I called him. It seemed like the thing to do at the time. I finally talked to Paul today. James is no friend of his. Apparently James is a joke among the serious researchers. He's been kicked off people's property in three states. We can only hope no one will let him camp on their place."

"Not so far. It seems James has come off so obnoxious that one lady sicced her dogs on him. That reminds me, Esther told me an odd story." I told them about the ducks.

Silence followed for a few moments, then Youdi said, "Things are really heating up out here, you had better keep a close watch on your animals."

When John came home, he and Curt hooked up the CBs at both cabins and made sure they worked properly before dark. John pretended to scoff at the idea, but I could tell that being able to communicate with another man gave him a sense of security. Curt was so grateful, he looked like he might cry. He and John talked several times on the CBs that evening, even though nothing happened.

John and I were asleep when the CB crackled to life at 1:30 a.m. Curt's terrified voice filled the room. "John, Sal.... are you there? Please be there. They're back. I don't know if I can handle this. Please answer."

John shook himself awake and grabbed the mike off the unit. "We're here. Try to calm down and tell me what's happening."

I could hear Curt sobbing.

"Oh God... I can hear them...feel them... I can't see anything, but I can hear them walking by the house. I can feel their footsteps. They're chattering like a bunch of Chinese men. Their steps are so heavy I can feel each one. God... they're by the front door. I can feel them on the other side. I'm so scared. What do I do if they come in?"

Curt was really losing it. I could hear Emily in the background trying to soothe him. "Are you still there, John? Please don't break off. I'm having trouble breathing. I can't seem to move. Oh God, I can hear them scratching on the door."

"We're right here. You aren't alone. Try to stay calm. Just keep talking to me."

"It's quiet. I don't know if that's better, or worse. Now they're moving again... Oh God, JOHN! They're coming toward your house. They're on the trail behind Youdi's cabin. If you look out the window, you'll see them. No, no, that's not right. We can't see them at all this time. I don't know if it's better to see them or not. Go to your window... now."

I heard Emily's voice come on the CB. John handed the mike to me and dove for the living room window. I knew I had nothing to fear from Skookum but Curt's terror was contagious. This wasn't the same as when I'd seen Skookum with Dream Walker. This was scary.

"Emily," I said. "Are you there?"

"Yeah, I...I just can't talk very well. My heart's racing. I've never heard anything like this. Their footsteps were so heavy I could feel them shaking the house. I can still feel them in the distance. Any time they should be coming by the corner of your house, then you'll..."

The waterbed began vibrating. My God, it was like a giant heartbeat. Whomp... whomp... whomp. I'd forgotten John wasn't there until I reached for him. The footsteps were only a wall away from me, heading toward the living room where John was sitting by the window. I could see him, frozen in place. Emily's voice came from a distance. "Sal... are you still there?"

I'd forgotten she was on the CB. The waterbed shook in rhythmic waves, even though the footsteps had passed. "Yes, I'm here. I'm a bit shaken. I'm hanging on to the side of the waterbed. They've passed my bedroom, and they're headed toward the living room. John's sitting by the window. He should be able to see them any minute."

"He won't see anything," Emily whispered.

"John," I called. No answer. "Emily, he won't talk to me. Oh God, they're by the window now. I can hear them."

"Go to the window," I heard Emily say. "Go to the window and see what you can see. But don't break contact."

Stretching the cord as far as I could, I tiptoed to John's side. I could feel the footsteps fading in the direction of the river. I shook John's shoulder. "John... what did you see? Talk to me."

John turned his head in my direction, and I looked into his eyes. In their depths I saw questions and wonder. Together we stared back out into the darkness.

"I saw nothing... and everything," he said.

Dozens of birds started chirping out in the night. They continued as I talked to Emily. I stayed on the CB until we both felt calmer. Then I hung it up and went in to where John was sitting. "Tell me what happened."

"I heard something huge coming toward the house. I could feel them just on the other side of the window. But... there was nothing there. I watched as the fir duff on the ground compressed in the shape of giant feet, then sprang back up as they walked on. I could feel them stomp... I could see the shape of their feet... but there was nothing there. I don't know how to deal with things like this. It did happen, didn't it?"

All I could do was nod. John the Skeptic was now John the Believer.

The next morning I called Youdi.

"Thank God for those CBs," I said. "We were all scared last night, especially Curt. I don't know what would have happened to him if he hadn't had John to talk to. It's completely different hearing about something and being a part of it. I know Skookum aren't violent to people, but something that massive right outside your window is terrifying. At least John believes us now. You should have seen his face."

From that night on, John's attitude was completely different. He could no longer deny what was going on; he didn't even try. He became eager to know if anything had happened while he was at work each day. His drinking ceased. Several times, I saw him reading my Bigfoot and UFO books.

Our relationship improved as well. He no longer seemed to resent the time I spent on research or my Native American ways. He took to wearing the slippers I had made him at every opportunity.

Chapter Twelve

...Therefore let the moon
Shine on thee in thy solitary walk;
And let the misty mountain-winds be free
To blow against thee...

If I should be where I no more can hear
Thy voice, nor catch from thy wild eyes these
gleams
Of past existence — wilt thou then forget
That on the banks of this delightful stream
We stood together

— *William Wordsworth*
"Tintern Abbey"

One night we got an excited call on the CB from Emily at about 9:00 o'clock. "Sal... are you there? Pick up, hurry. Go look out toward the road."

I ran to the front window and pushed aside the curtain. I thought I saw very bright car headlights moving away from me down the road toward Esther's house.

"Did you see it? Or was it going too fast?"

"I saw a car, or something, leaving. Is that what you mean?"

"It wasn't a car. It was a huge, white light that came through our yard. I looked out the kitchen window and it blinded me. It stayed in one place for a minute then cruised slowly across the yard out to the road. I could see it through the trees heading past your house. It lit up everything over here like daylight. I'm surprised you didn't see it."

"I was reading. I thought it was just a car with its brights on. Did it make any noise?"

"No, no noise at all. It was like a big searchlight, but it wasn't attached to anything. It just floated through the yard."

"Well, it couldn't have been a helicopter. They make a lot of noise, and there are too many power lines and trees along the road for one to fly that low."

"No, it wasn't anything like that. It was just a big light. I felt like it was watching me. I'll call if it comes again."

There were no more calls that night, which was a good thing because I wasn't there. I wondered what would happen if Curt or Emily tried to contact me when I was with Dream Walker. Would I be able to hear the CB from wherever I was in the past?

Dream Walker's thoughts came immediately when I closed my eyes. "Tonight, we must have wings on our feet. Our time together grows short and there is much I must tell you."

Contrary to his words, Dream Walker and I traveled a great distance in silence. The evening fog embraced the forest like a gray lover. Drops of moisture clung to each leaf and frond then fell with the sound of soft kisses to the duff on the forest floor. After many twists and turns, Dream

Walker slowed his pace. I had the feeling our destination was near.

The old man moved with reverence through the dripping trees. It seemed we were on a journey that held great significance for my guide.

I almost lost my balance when Dream Walker ducked under a massive fallen cedar then rounded a sharp curve. I smelled smoke and heard a faint chanting. What I had mistaken for the rhythmic beating of my own heart grew in intensity as we neared a small clearing.

An old man sat by a guttering fire. His long hair hung loose and, except for two yellow streaks, it was pure white. Wrinkles were etched deeply into what I could see of his face. With bowed head, his voice carried softly on the damp breeze. His gnarled hands kept beat with the words. "Tahmanhawis Skookum... kloshe-nanitch wehut-sag ha lic... Ole klutchman Sallal cly tum tum... Youtle tum tum yahwa alhupso sikhs."

I looked at Dream Walker. As our eyes met, something shifted in the air. The clearing became electric as I chanted along in the tongue of my day. "Guardian spirit of Skookum... be careful on the trail to Heaven ... this old woman, Sallal cries in her heart... joy in the beyond, secret friend."

And then I knew. This was not a man. This Shaman helping Skookum on his final journey was my namesake, Sallal. I should have guessed from the yellow streaks in her hair. When she raised her head I saw the pendant that hung from her neck, and mine, by the light of the fire.

Dream Walker glanced to his left at a thick stand of fir. A dark shape stood hidden there: a huge shape, taller than a man. As my eyes adjusted to the darkness outside the clearing, I saw many such shapes standing like small trees. The hair stood up on my body when I realized we were surrounded.

"Do not fear, my friend. One of their kind is leaving his body. We are all here to witness the passing of his spirit. He is the Skookum who saved you from the water so long ago."

The chanting and drumming became progressively stronger until it reached a crescendo, then stopped. The circle of shapes melted into the forest as if they had never been there. They had taken the body of their comrade with them. The Shaman slumped over her drum and light dimmed in the clearing. Screams echoed back and forth down the canyon, sounding like a mother giving birth.

Dream Walker and I retraced our steps until we came to the whale rock. We sat on its great back. Dream Walker's yellowed eyes gazed off into the sky above the ridge. "Soon you will no longer walk in two worlds, Sallal. I have shown you your past so you will have the knowledge to change the future. If anyone can make a difference, it is you and the others who have been gathered. Soon more will follow. Each will be given a piece of the puzzle. Only by being pure of spirit and working as one, will the pieces fit. If only one is not true to the others, all will fail.

"I learned long ago that some pasaiooks are pure in spirit, but there are many more who are not. Some would hunt Skookum to kill them for their own gain. Even now, the forces of evil and greed hover near.

"Remember all I have shown you and teach your young ones. I will not be here to remind you. Make sure the children believe in what they cannot touch or see. Then if you fail to solve the puzzle, perhaps one of them can.

"To one of you a girl child has been born. She has the sunbeams in her hair. One day I will come to her as I have come to you. She too will learn the ways of our people and of Skookum.

"Much time will pass, and this child will take many false paths before she wears the pendant of Sallal. But one day she will walk in the footsteps of Skookum and gaze at the autumn star."

Night had fallen, and Dream Walker motioned to the sky over the ridge. The huge white light we had seen before hung there like a floodlight in the sky. "Tenas cole illahee ... tsiltsil chil chil. The autumn star... it is my campfire. I have enjoyed my time with you, Sallal. I will return to sit by my campfire now before your face changes in the light of morning."

And with that, he was gone.

I awoke bereft at the loss of my friend and mentor. I sat on the edge of the bed and gazed deeply into the depths of the green, streaked mirror hoping for a sign of his presence. Only my own tear-streaked face looked back at me. I wondered why he had chosen me as his pupil. If, in fact, I had been the medicine woman, Sallal, in another time, I felt I could sure use some magical help now. I certainly didn't feel capable of solving the puzzle that had been set before me. I wasn't even sure exactly what the puzzle was. I reached for the pendant at my throat. Could this piece of antique jewelry, passed down from my mother, really have mystical power as Dream Walker claimed? It hadn't left my neck since I received it. I would make doubly sure I wore it in the days to come. "I miss you already, Dream Walker," I said.

"Who is Dream Walker?"

I froze. Then I realized when Autumn came into the room I had been talking to my reflection in the mirror. I must get a grip. I was back in my own time, not with Dream Walker in the past. "No one, honey. I was just talking to myself. Let's go have breakfast."

The phone rang as we entered the kitchen. The bright, cheery voice of Youdi lifted my mood.

"I just finished talking to Paul in California," she said. "He's making plans to come up. There will be four of them: Paul's wife, Hilda, and another couple, Toby and Laura. Toby is a psychic who has helped Paul with his investigations over the years. He should be helpful in getting some answers."

I thought of Dream Walker's recent words, *"Some of you have already been gathered. More will follow. If even one is not true to the others, all will fail."*

The first order of business was to somehow get rid of "Bwana" James. I thought, "Speak of the devil," when he pulled into our driveway a short while later. Rather than let him in, I walked out to meet him. Emily, Curt, and their boys arrived at the same moment. Rain began in huge splatting drops. I had no choice but to ask them all in.

John came out of the bathroom wrapped in a towel. It was Sunday and my whole family was home. John went to get dressed while Autumn took the boys to her room to play. I went to put on coffee. James grabbed Curt's hand to shake it like they were long lost friends. Curt yanked back his hand and looked at it like it was dirty. I could see dislike emanating like daggers from his eyes. Although an uncomfortable silence followed, James seemed not to notice. He removed his pith helmet and opened his oversized backpack, placing a sheaf of papers on the kitchen table. "I've brought along some articles on a number of other sightings I've investigated. I thought you would all be interested in seeing some of my work."

No one commented.

"Anyway, I've also brought some high tech equipment that I feel sure will aid us in our, uh, search."

Emily picked up one of the reports. James began explaining an infrared scope to the men. While their attention was captured, I took the phone to the bedroom and called Youdi.

"Sal? I didn't expect to hear from you so soon. Has something happened?"

"I'm afraid so. Bwana James showed up just after you called. Emily and her family are here, too. James brought a stack of articles and a bag of expensive equipment to dazzle the natives. I don't know how to get rid of this guy. I wouldn't have let him in but we were all getting soaked standing in the yard. I asked them inside rather than let James get Emily and Curt alone at their house. Curt really despises James. I'm afraid there might be trouble. Curt's not too stable these days. What did Paul have to say about James?"

"Nothing good, I'm afraid. He said to try to discourage him, but be careful. He's been known to become violent when he doesn't get his way. Several people have had to escort him off their property at gunpoint because he wouldn't leave them alone. Keep everything as calm as you can. I'll be right out." She hung up.

"Oh swell," I thought. 'This lunatic is parked at my kitchen table, and my neighbor looks ready to punch him. Now what?'

Curt seemed to have mellowed some by the time I returned to the kitchen. James had apparently captured his attention with his expensive toys. John, too, seemed spellbound as he watched the man demonstrate an automatic movie camera with a night scope.

Emily was deep in a report. She jumped when I asked her to come help me with lunch. I took her aside and told her what Youdi had said. James was playing an annoying tape of babies crying. He claimed it drew Bigfoot in.

Emily looked freaked. "Oh God. How do we get rid of him? Curt has a terrible temper and if James says anything wrong, he'll blow."

"Calm down, Emily. We'll do our best to keep them talking until your mom gets here. Let's feed everyone then send all the kids to your house. Krista's old enough to keep an eye on them. Then I guess we just hope for the best."

Lunch was a strained affair. Once the excitement of James' toys had worn off, Curt's expression returned to that of a cornered lion. He bristled with hostility. James seemed oblivious as he nattered on, becoming more boastful and obnoxious by the moment. It was three hours before Youdi burst in.

"Hi everyone. Sorry I'm late, but my car wouldn't start."

James looked at us like, "What's going on? She wasn't invited."

Apparently he had spoken to Paul and he was aware she had talked to Paul also. He knew his reputation had just taken a nosedive.

Youdi asked Curt and Emily if they would help her unload her car. She planned to spend the night. After they'd gone, James started in where he'd left off. John interrupted. When he spoke, I realized he must have heard me talking to Youdi on the phone.

"Well James, it's been real, but I've got a lot of things to do." He began stuffing James' things into his backpack.

James grabbed it, looking dumbfounded. "I don't believe this. You're asking me to leave? But, I'm just getting started. I haven't even told you about the time I single-handedly..."

John picked up the helmet and popped it onto the startled man's head, then turned him toward the door.

"But, but... we were getting along fine. Why have you turned on me? You haven't even told me where I can sleep."

I could tell John was becoming irritated. "You are <u>NOT</u> staying here. What gave you that idea?"

James' face was purple. "You people called *me*, remember? I've given you hours of my valuable time and now you think I'm just going to leave? Well, forget it. I'm not..."

John grabbed him at his waist and shoulders with both hands, propelling him out the door, then across the driveway to his van. James sputtered obscenities all the way. A flash of brilliant color caught my eye. Esther and Blackjack came around the front of the van. Blackjack lunged and caught James by the leg, gumming him viciously.

James tried in vain to kick him loose.

"Sic him, Blackjack!" Esther yelled. "Good dog."

James snarled at Esther then turned to John. He tried to look menacing, but it didn't work so well with a dog hanging from his leg. "How dare you, you pathetic yokel. Damn dog! Let go of me! If you think I'm leaving this river, you're wrong. If we don't get scientific proof, no one will believe you."

"That's what you don't seem to understand. We don't care if anyone believes us. Now get out of here and don't come back."

Esther called Blackjack off and I heard a noise by Youdi's cabin. There stood Emily, Curt, and Youdi. Curt had a murderous look in his eye and a shotgun hugged to his chest.

James hopped in his van and peeled out of the driveway. We could hear him muttering to himself as he drove off. "I'll be around, no matter what you say. I'll get my Bigfoot."

Esther reached down and took a piece of James' pants from Blackjack's mouth. "I hope we've seen the last of that jerk."

I had my doubts.

John gave Curt a satisfied look. "You should have seen the rack of guns our 'peaceful' friend has in his van."

"I've talked to everyone on the road," Youdi said. "Not one of them will let him stay on their land. What about Pete and Janet, Sal?"

"Pete ran him off last week. James won't have access to that side of the river or the ridge."

Later that evening, Emily's excited voice came over the CB. "You and John should come see what's happening in the sky over the ridge. It's beautiful. Stop by Mom's cabin and bring her, too, please."

We slipped on our coats and picked up Youdi at her cabin. Emily walked us out to the side of her house and pointed to the sky across the river. Above the ridge, in a cloudless sky full of stars, was the white light. It was the size of a beacon. Dream Walker's campfire.

"Tenas cole illahee tsil tsil chil chil," Youdi whispered in awe, as she dropped to her knees in the grass.

For a moment I could hardly breathe. "What did you say?"

"It is an old legend. My grandmother told it to me when I was a girl. What you see is the autumn star. The old ones claimed it was the campfire of a powerful Shaman named Dream Walker. This Shaman claimed he had acquired his powers and knowledge from other Shaman while they journeyed together in dreams, sort of an early Edgar Cayce.

"Throughout Native American history there have been many who were visited by this Shaman in their dreams. Dream Walker has been called by many names but I believe they are all the same person. There was once a great medicine woman in this valley that journeyed with Dream Walker. Her name was Sallal. My grandmother told me Sallal had a special friendship with a Skookum who saved her from drowning.

"I have scanned the skies since I was young, but until now I have never seen this autumn star."

I, too, had knelt on the ground as I listened to Youdi. The others joined us as we watched the huge light. Suddenly, it began pulsing and turned red, blue, green, and yellow in rapid succession, but it remained stationary. It repeated this display. Then Youdi cried out. “Look, there’s a light on the ridge!”

We watched, hypnotized, as the big light began moving in slow circles. It would dim and blink out, then reappear in a flash of brilliance a short distance away. Then it returned to its original position. The small light on the ridge blinked furiously then rose to meet it. Five or six small, colored lights appeared beneath the large one as it began to move in jerky jumps to the right and left above them. Then the colored lights disappeared in a blink and the autumn star hung motionless in the sky. All the other stars were lackluster compared to its brilliance.

John and I went home after a few minutes to continue watching from the couch in the living room. Though we could see it through the trees out the back window, nothing else happened. The autumn star remained in one place, while the rest of the night sky moved slowly past. I had taken my glasses off to rub my eyes when John yelled. “WOW, did you see that?”

Of course, I hadn’t.

John described a shooting star the size of the moon. He said it was bright yellow or orange, with a long tail. We discovered the next day that Youdi’s son Mic had seen the same thing at the exact time, in the sky at his house almost twenty miles away.

We watched the autumn star and the accompanying smaller lights for several nights to come. During this time, some of John’s earlier skepticism resurfaced. “Maybe it’s just a bunch of stars,” he said.

John decided to prove it to himself one way or another. He made a mark on the window, figuring if the display had moved slightly during the night it was a natural phenomenon moving with the rotation of the earth. If it stayed in the same place, it was something else. His theory didn't take into account all the unstar-like things it had already done, but I didn't point that out.

When he sat down later to check his mark with the lights, there was nothing in the sky but a million small stars. The display of lights hadn't moved; it had disappeared. John was speechless. The next night the entire display was back in place, exactly on John's mark.

"Oh, ye of little faith," I whispered in his ear.

On our way to bed the screams started.

"What in the hell was that?" John said.

"It's exactly what you think it is. I'm glad you've finally heard them."

That night, Emily called on the CB to say she had seen the big light in her yard again. When she switched off the house lights, it had zoomed across her field of vision and disappeared into the trees across the road.

When John came home from work the next day, he was scowling. A man at work had shown him an article from the Tacoma newspaper reporting that two men had seen a Bigfoot on the banks of the Carbon River during the recent flood. One of the men's daughters had seen a Bigfoot at the same spot on another occasion.

I could feel blood pounding in my temples. James had written the article.

"The guy at work who showed me this asked if I knew anything about it. He knows we live on the river. I told him it's a long river. 'Besides,' I told him, 'I don't believe in all that crap. Do you?' " John gave me a crooked smile.

I hugged him. "Thank you."

His expression changed. "If I ever see that James jerk around here again I'll stuff him in a hollow log and let Bigfoot find him."

Chapter Thirteen

They followed from the snowy bank
Those footmarks, one by one,
Into the middle of the plank;
And further there were none!

— *William Wordsworth*
"Lucy Gray"

Spring had come to the woods again. Tiny buds draped the maples in a veil of chartreuse. The trees were filled with twittering birds until Autumn and I reached the beginning of Youdi's path. Animals seemed to avoid this area. As we walked through the ancient, decaying logs, I realized there were never any spider webs here to block our way. Elsewhere, at this time of the morning, I had to carry a stick to clear the way.

I had also noticed that the chickens and ducks avoided this place. This rotting paradise that should have been a gourmet delight for my bug-eating birds was off limits.

Once I began paying attention, it occurred to me that this path through the center of the logs wasn't overgrown from disuse; rather it was well worn, as though traveled frequently. I found one area, then another, where the soft logs had been crushed to sawdust. Curious now, I climbed up. About ten feet off the ground was a moss-lined alcove that appeared to be the resting-place of something large. When I pulled myself up a bit higher, I felt my stomach clench. The spot afforded a direct view of our living room window.

I climbed back down and went on to the next spot where something had crushed the logs. Another moss-lined bower was perched on the opposite side of the trail. It looked into the living room of Emily and Curt's house, where they slept. Both hidey-holes were well used and had the faint skunky smell I was familiar with. Autumn and I ran to get Emily.

When she saw the viewing stations, she went limp and sat down. "No wonder I always feel like I'm being watched."

After we called Youdi, we decided to bait the trail by putting out some of the kid's toys and various tidbits of food. Autumn donated "Dapper Dan," her favorite doll. She hoped that would get a young Bigfoot to come play. We added some of Greg and Randy's toys and a mirror from an old compact. Food treats consisted of raisins, a couple of hard-boiled eggs, some crackers, and two wrapped packets of freezer-burned rabbit. We divided this and placed half in each of the hiding places we had found.

We checked the bait daily but it remained undisturbed.

On Sunday, John's friend Greg came to visit. Since he lived out on the coast in Gig Harbor, we hadn't seen him in some time. After dinner we were sitting in the living room, filling Greg in on all the odd things that had happened since we moved here. He asked me where we had seen the light displays. When I pointed to the window, he looked out and jumped off the couch. "Some big guy just ran past that white thing out there!"

The "white thing" proved to be Youdi's well house at the beginning of her path. Greg was really spooked and left almost immediately.

At 1:00 a.m. the same night, Curt's frantic voice came over the CB. He and Emily were hearing whistles and moaning outside. While he was describing this, heavy footsteps began by Youdi's path. John and I crept out of bed and sat on the couch for about an hour but we neither saw nor heard anything else. If anything, the night was too quiet: not peaceful, but a waiting silence that caused me to hold my breath. Only once was this silence broken by a loud "CAW" that sounded like an angry crow.

The next morning, Emily said that they had arrived home about 11:00 p.m. and were greeted by a chorus of chirping birds. A couple of hours later they awoke to low, moaning sounds outside the window closest to Youdi's cabin. That turned into whistling and noises like teenage girls giggling. Emily looked confused when I said we had felt footsteps, but heard nothing but that one "CAW."

When we went to check the bait on Youdi's path there was nothing left but the papers used to wrap the rabbit. Both packets had been carefully unwrapped, not torn open.

Autumn was happy to find that her doll had been taken. To her, it meant that a young Bigfoot had accepted her gift.

While we were discussing the possibilities of the bait being taken, loud pounding noises erupted in the direction of the river. The ground vibrated beneath our feet. We gathered the children and hurried toward the sounds. We were breathing hard when we paused on the levee road to get our bearings. The rumbling, pounding, machinery sounds of a large factory came from the ground we stood on and echoed off the canyon walls.

"This is crazy," I said. "There's nothing within thirty miles that could make those noises."

Emily sniffed the wind. "Something's burning. It smells like hot metal or melted wiring."

We scanned the canyon but could see nothing unusual. The odors decreased as we headed home but our eyes still watered. Every so often the ground shook, as if something extremely heavy had been dropped. The sounds continued for several hours, then stopped abruptly. It was as though a shift had ended.

When John came home, I told him what had happened. We walked to the river. The noises had long since ceased but the burning smell lingered and John pinched his nose. "Whatever it is, it reminds me of Detroit. I haven't smelled anything like that since we moved out here. And the sounds came from where?"

"Everywhere. We couldn't pinpoint a direction. Whatever they were, they shook the ground."

"Well, maybe it'll happen again while I'm home."

It didn't that day.

But the next morning, after John left for work, the rumblings started again and lasted the entire day. At times, the smell was overpowering. A faint haze hung over the canyon.

John and I walked to the river later that afternoon. I saw the disbelieving look on his face when a rumble caused the ground to shake. He steadied himself on a nearby tree. "I thought you were exaggerating. I have no idea what could be causing this."

That night, the waterbed was still vibrating from the noises when the CB crackled to life. Emily's voice roused me from sleep and filled the room. “The orange ball followed us home. It kept pace with our truck all the way from the fish hatchery outside of town. It was over the river but I could see it through the trees. Curt got spooked a couple of times and tried to outrun it but it just sped up. I had to make him slow down so we wouldn’t crash. I was scared. It’s beautiful, though, about the size of a basketball, with a glow around it. After we turned into our driveway I watched it jet off up river.”

When Youdi arrived the next morning, she told us that Mic had called all freaked out the night before. On his way home from town two orange “fireballs” had swooped down on his car. He was so startled he’d had trouble braking. He said he almost ended up in a ditch trying to avoid them. After he stopped, they streaked off in the sky in our direction. Youdi was amazed when Emily told her one had followed her and Curt home.

The rumbling noises began again while we were talking and we filled Youdi in on our way down the trail. She said they sounded like the same noises she had heard in the past. A search of the area provided no clues as to what was causing the sounds and smell. We were all baffled.

Youdi had planned a surprise outing for the day. She had brought along a picnic lunch and her teenaged son, Joey, whom I had never met before. He usually stayed in town with his dad. Youdi told us that we would be picnicking at a place she referred to as “Grandmother’s Cave.” It was located up the mountain, a few miles outside the town of Wilkeson.

Curt had taken the day off work, so he drove their truck. Everyone else piled into Youdi's car and she led the way. While we drove, Youdi filled me in on some of her grandmother's colorful childhood.

"Back in those days, the place we are going to was a working stone quarry. Grandmother's family lived in a small cabin on one side of a nearby pond. The local bootlegger lived on the other side. Between their houses was a bridge where the moonshiner hid his finished product. The job of distributing it fell to the girl who would one day be my grandmother. In those days, children just did as they were told.

"When the newest batch of 'shine' was bottled, my grandmother was handed a battered suitcase and told to fill it with bottles from beneath the bridge. Then she would walk to the town of Wilkeson to make her deliveries. It was a long, tiring trip for a girl. She had been instructed to never allow anyone to help her carry the suitcase. She had also been taught to carry her burden carefully so the bottles wouldn't clink and so the suitcase didn't seem heavy. Grandmother said she made these illegal deliveries until she was grown."

Youdi also shared what her great grandfather had told his daughter about the cave we were going to visit. "Grandmother said her father had warned her to never go near the cave because it was where *Tsiatko Skookum* lived. He said these beings were night-roaming demons that would take her. She would never be seen again. My grandmother avoided the cave her entire life. She said she believed her father because of the screams she heard coming from that direction at night."

Youdi, on the other hand, couldn't wait to explore its depths. She had brought along flashlights and ropes for our descent.

When we arrived at our destination, her hopes were soon crushed. We could see the remains of the two cabins and the bridge but not much else. In the forty-odd years since Youdi had been here, the pond had been reduced to a stinking swamp. The stone quarry had long since been abandoned, but not before the entrance to the cave was blasted shut.

Massive boulders blocked the way where half of the cliff had come down. The place had the eerie silence of a ghost town. Not a bird could be heard in the surrounding forest of huge trees. The sun shone weakly when the rolling clouds parted and rain looked imminent. We spread our lunch on a boulder and ate in silence.

Curt and Joey climbed to the far side of the rock pile after lunch to see if they could find another entrance to the cave. The women and children waited on the picnic rock, sending out hoots and whistles to while away the time until the others returned. Half an hour later, we heard Joey shout, "Hey, what's this?"

We watched as he bent to scoop something from a rock. He brought back a wet, white pile of what looked like vomit. It was balanced on the end of a stick. Woven into the mess were white hairs about three inches long. Emily said they were the same color as the young Skookum she had seen in her yard. We dropped the mass into an empty sandwich bag so Youdi could take it home to send to Paul in California. She said she would attach a note asking if Skookum got hairballs. We all laughed.

We arrived home to find James' van parked in my driveway. He was sitting on the porch like he owned the place.

"What in the hell do you want?" I said.

He just smiled. "I thought I'd stop by to see if anything new is happening in the area. The newspaper asked me to check."

I saw red. "Do you actually think anyone around here would share anything with you after you went to the paper? You were told last time not to come back. Get in your van and *leave*."

James smirked and got in my face. "And who's going to make me? It's a weekday. Both John and Curt are at work. I figure I've got a couple of hours to look around before they come home." He turned and bumped into Curt's massive form.

"I don't think so, you son of a bitch," Curt growled.

James' face lost all its color. Curt had murder in his eyes and a rifle in his hands. It was pointed at James' chest. "If I were you, I'd do as she said. Turn real slow and walk to your van." Curt poked the rifle at him. "If you show up here again, I'll drop you where you stand. Then I'll load you in your own van and drive you up the mountain where I'll throw your body over a cliff for the buzzards to eat. Now, get the hell out of here!"

James wisely believed him, because he did exactly as he was told. He drove away without saying a word. Curt turned and disappeared into the trees. I was grateful, but couldn't help thinking, "I'm sure glad he's not mad at me."

At 1:00 a.m. Curt's voice on the CB woke us. He seemed strangely calm when he said he could hear heavy footsteps on Youdi's path again. He said the Skookum seemed to be mimicking the hoots and whistles we had been making at the stone quarry that day. I listened for a long time, but could hear nothing.

Youdi arrived the next day with her husband, Bud, to spend the weekend at the cabin. This was only the second time I had ever met Bud. He was a tall, thin *pasaiook*. He seemed nice, but he appeared to have no interest in Indian ways or Skookum. He also didn't seem to have much interest in getting to know any of us. Bud stayed inside their cabin and read most of the weekend. Youdi said he had been badly burned at work. I supposed that accounted for his reluctance to socialize.

It had been raining for almost a week when Youdi and Bud showed up. I had spent most of the last six months cooped up in my small cabin because of the rain. I was tired of staying in. Tomorrow I was going out, even if I had to wear hip boots.

When I woke up, hail was pelting the roof like a machine gun. It soon stopped and turned to rain again. The sun had just peaked through threatening clouds when I heard a knock on the door. Youdi's head peeked inside, "Come on, let's get outside. We'll walk to the end of the road. I'll show you my other piece of property. Bring a camera if you have one. There's an old railroad

The end of the road

trestle up the canyon I've always wanted a picture of."

I told John where I was going, grabbed my coat and the camera, and escaped before anything could stop me. Youdi was waiting on the road. I took a deep, cleansing breath as we started off. I felt like I'd been released from prison.

We walked in silence for about half a mile. It was damp and cold but I didn't care. The only sounds were birds and the rain dripping from the trees. Youdi set a brisk pace. We passed a couple of houses where the residents were snuggled inside. Today, I was glad I wasn't one of them.

"This is the first time I've ever walked down the road farther than Emily's house," I said.

Youdi laughed.

"No, really. I've walked with you by the river and in the woods but I've never had any reason to come this way. I didn't even know you owned more property out here."

"Bud and I have ten acres down here. Before the flood, there were a couple of nice ponds on it where beavers had dammed up the creek. Both the ponds and the beavers are gone now. We were going to build on the site but the flood changed our minds. Only three retired couples and a single man live toward this end of the road. It's peaceful up here."

The further we walked, the fewer signs of civilization we saw. Youdi pointed to the trees on our left and said we were passing her property. I could hear a small creek rushing through the underbrush.

About a mile further, the road dead-ended in a black and white striped barricade. I could see deep ruts where four-wheel drive vehicles had plowed through the mud and gone around in the past but none of the tracks were recent.

"From here on there is only a dirt road that is almost impassable, even in summer," Youdi said. "The railroad used to come through here from Carbanado and Wilkeson but it was washed out long ago. Years later the rest of the tracks were taken out and the road was built. After the jeep road, there is only an animal trail leading down a steep cliff to a nice, sandy beach. From there we can see the remains of the old trestle. I've always wanted a picture of it."

The jeep road was about a quarter mile long. It was more a pond than a road. Some of the puddles looked deep enough to have fish in them. It was obvious no vehicles had come this way for a long time. We walked beside the so-called road through tall grass and berry vines. A filtered green light shone wistfully through the tall trees. A sweet fragrance filled my nose as we trod on the wild mint and new violets that carpeted the ground.

The jeep road ended as abruptly as the paved road had. The barricade here was dense forest.

Time seemed to thicken and slow around me. Tall trees stretched arms skyward, offering their prayers to the Great Spirit. I felt Dream Walker's presence near. I stood still and willed the past to come... but, of course, it would not. Dream Walker was gone and with him my link to the tunnel of time. I called out, but only the echo of my cry answered. I was a lone traveler in a small green world of sights and sounds. All was quiet, except for my labored breathing. Then the sun broke through the clouds. Its presence failed to coax even one bird to sing. Youdi's voice came to me, but the eerie silence of my surroundings persisted.

"Sal... Sal, answer me. Are you okay?"

"I'm okay." As I struggled back to my senses, I noticed that ancient cedars and gnarled maples spread a dense canopy of branches over the spot where we stood. "Sorry Youdi, I was just thinking of a friend. He's gone now."

"Let's go before it starts raining again."

Youdi marched down the trail and ducked under a sodden limb. Still disoriented, I followed as best I could, fending off wet branches that slapped my face and slimy ferns that soaked my pant legs. I was almost a foot taller than Youdi and I found the going rough. Branches she slipped under were face-level for me. Finally, one whacked me so hard I landed in the mud.

"Wait, Youdi!" I yelled. "I've got to rest a minute."

She must have been too far ahead to hear my plea. I found myself alone in the woods. I scrambled to my feet, wiping the sticky mud from my hands. The silence was unnerving. It was like being in a tomb.

The hair rose on my neck and I ran down the path in a panic. I had the same feeling I'd had on my first day in the valley... something was close behind.

Panting and disheveled, I reached the trail's end. Youdi sat on a rock waiting. "What kept you, Sallal?" She said, smiling, her round eyes alight with secret glee.

I was stunned. "You <u>know</u>?!"

"What? Of your travels with the Dream Walker? Of course. You wear the necklace of the one with sunbeams in her hair. I saw it the day we met. But it will be our secret. We don't need to speak of it again. Come, let's go down to the beach. I have a feeling we have been called here."

I was so taken aback I hadn't even noticed my surroundings. To the right of the rock Youdi sat on rose a sheer cliff. Below us the rocks jutted out only a couple of feet, then cascaded to the beach below in a jumble of debris. We were standing at the top of a landslide. Far below lay a pristine, sandy beach in a half moon shape.

Youdi made her way easily along the narrow shelf. There was no way my big feet would fit on that goat trail. I decided to descend the twenty-foot drop by climbing over boulders. By doing so, I would end up at the other end of the beach. My plan worked well until the boulders ended about halfway down. I had no choice but to slide the remaining distance in the mud. Down I went, tumbling and skidding. I landed with a loud plop in the wet sand. Youdi rushed to my side, doubled over with laughter.

"Not very graceful, my friend. You look like you've been mud wrestling. Are you hurt?"

I shook my head. The only thing wounded was the camera. It was covered with mud. John would not be pleased. The camera was his baby. I tried to wipe the mud off with my shirt, but that made it worse. "So much for your trestle picture, Youdi. This thing is probably ruined."

Youdi wasn't paying any attention to me. She was staring at the wet sand by our feet. Her voice came out hushed and reverent. "Sal... look."

My eyes went to where she was pointing but, at first, I didn't realize what I was seeing. "It's freezing out here. Why would anyone be stupid enough to hike all the way here then climb down that cliff barefoot?" Then it dawned on me. "Oh my God, those aren't made by people! Look at the width. It's Skookum. These are Bigfoot tracks!"

She only nodded.

The beach was covered with fresh, deep tracks in every direction. We had ruined several by arriving. I was so excited I sputtered, "Oh... jeez, what should we do first? Let's see... I'll try to clean the camera. We should take all the pictures we can. This is amazing! I wonder if anyone has ever found this many prints at one time."

"Be careful where you step, Sal. We don't want to ruin any more."

We tiptoed between footprints to the water's edge. I wiped down the camera, being careful not to get water inside. Then we inspected the beach. Wherever we looked, perfect, crisp prints,

Youdi's hand next to the crippled print

some as deep as an inch, were pressed into the wet sand. I noticed that our own shoes barely made a dent.

Some prints crossed over others and were distorted, but most were of such quality it was difficult to decide what to photograph. We counted over fifty in all. Several things became apparent as we inspected the beach. A single creature wasn't responsible for the prints. We found at least three distinctly different shapes. One had been crippled, the print curved and sadly misshapen. None of the prints had claw marks. This ruled out a bear or any other large animal. The prints weren't the eighteen to twenty inches I had read about. These averaged eleven to twelve inches long and five to six inches wide. The crippled prints were the only exception. They were about the same length, but narrower.

The tracks had been made within the last hour, since the rain

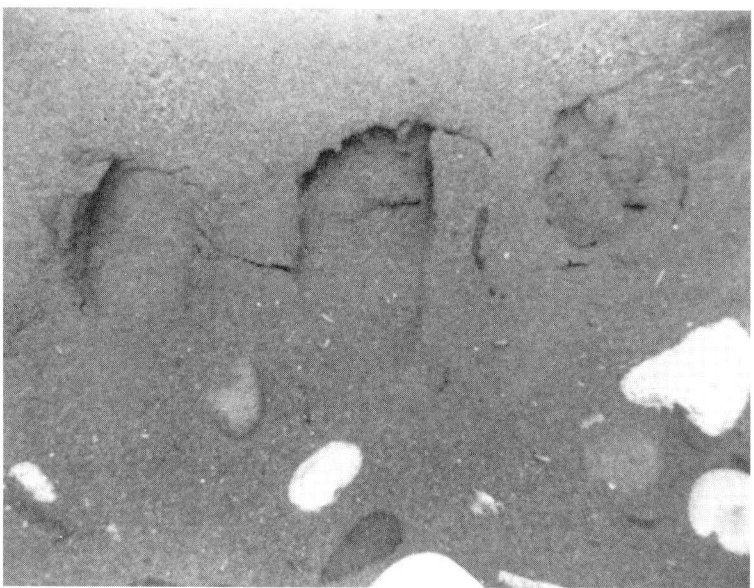

Sali's size 10 boot print (left) next to a Bigfoot print

had stopped. They were still crisp around the edges.

We chose several of the best and I snapped pictures until the film ran out.

“Now,” Youdi whispered, “let’s hope the camera worked.”

I smiled, and turned to her. “Why are you whispering?”

“I don’t know. It seemed like the thing to do. You know, like in church?”

I had to agree.

Somehow I managed to scale the cliff and navigate my way along the goat trail. On the way home, it began hailing again.

Once home, I changed clothes and drove to the town of Puyallup, some twenty miles away, to deposit the film for processing. The girl said it would be ready in three to four days. She agreed to call me as soon as it came in. While in town, I purchased some plaster of Paris to make casts of some of the prints.

That night, Curt called on the CB to say the big light had come back. It had circled their yard three times then headed off toward the river. I ran to the window just in time to see the woods out back lit up like day. The light was moving in the direction of the highway. I wondered if Shannon would see it from her bedroom window.

Curt’s voice was almost normal now when he called to report an occurrence. Perhaps it was because so many things had happened they had become commonplace. We no longer wondered *if* something would happen, but *when*. There was still the question *why*. What was the thread that connected so many seemingly unrelated phenomena?

We hoped Paul's psychic friend, Toby, could help put some of these things in perspective. I had found cases in the books I'd read similar to some of the occurrences around here but nothing had come close to explaining the combination. I had begun writing to Paul over the past few weeks. He had sent me masses of newspaper clippings about Bigfoot and UFO sightings from all over the country. I had sent him a copy of, "My Secret Friend," the children's book I'd written about Bigfoot.

John butchered more rabbits the next morning. When he brought in carcasses I thanked the rabbits for giving their lives so that we might live, then I cut and wrapped the meat for the freezer and prepared the hides. The two older girls always found somewhere else to go on this bloody day, but Autumn watched with profound interest, often helping when she could.

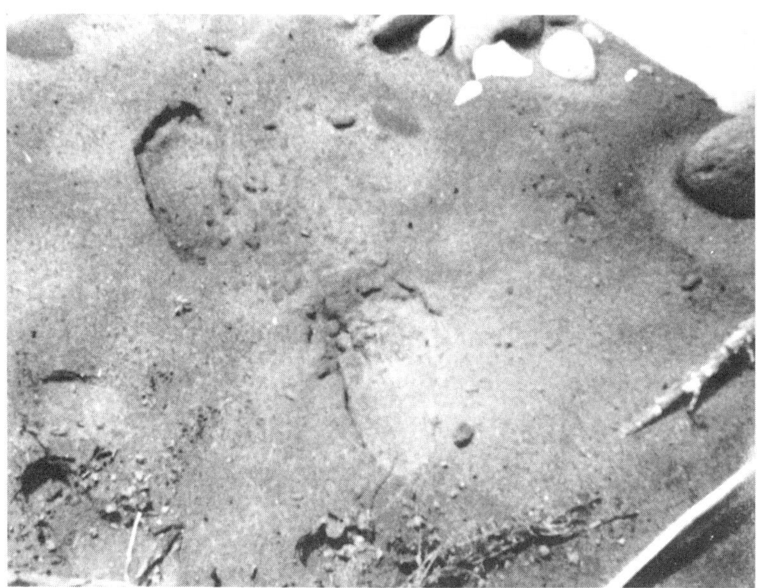

Part of a row of prints

This time I saved the entrails and scraps, wrapping them in several layers of butcher paper. I taped each packet securely. Autumn and I walked to Youdi's path and deposited one in each of the hollowed out places high in the logs. Both spots had been used recently. I could see places where chunks of wood had been ripped loose and the air was ripe with the odor I knew well.

Youdi's path was a fairyland once again. Delicate leaves and fronds of renewed life hovered about dead twigs of winter like a haze. Soon they would explode into the tender greenery that decorated the forest until the next frost. Spring was my favorite time of year... a new beginning, with months of promise ahead. I said a silent thanks to the Great Spirit for my life in this valley.

I felt the ground tremble and smelled heat as Autumn and I walked to the river. New vegetation had sprung up like magic, hiding the devastation of a few months ago. The land now looked much as it had before the flood. We saw Youdi at the foot of her trail and she hiked up river with us.

John agreed to keep an eye on Autumn while Youdi and I drove to the end of the road. We took along the tools and plaster to make casts of the Bigfoot prints on the beach. We parked at the barricade and walked through the silent woods to the cliff.

I swallowed my fear and followed Youdi down the goat trail to the beach. We were dismayed when we discovered the rain had destroyed every print. They were nothing but shapeless dents in the sand.

Though we searched the entire beach, we couldn't find one example intact enough to make a cast. We really didn't care for our own benefit, but Paul was eager to have a cast for his collection.

Youdi and I were standing by the water's edge when the first rock hit me on the shoulder. Before we had time to absorb what was going on, rocks came flying from all along the other side of the river. We ran, hollering, to the safety of the cliff and looked back as the last few stones thudded to the sand. I rubbed my shoulder where the first rock had hit.

"What the hell was that?"

"I think we are being told, not so politely, to leave," she said.

We took the hint.

On the way back, we talked about the possibility of pranksters having thrown the rocks. There was no road on that side of the river; no access at all, except through Pete and Janet's property. Their place was at least six miles downstream. The first town upstream was Wilkeson, about twenty miles away, and no one could have crossed over from our side; the river was too swollen from the recent rains.

The rocks had been tossed from several directions at once. They hadn't been thrown with enough force to injure us or we both would have been a bloody mess. Rather, they had been tossed into the air to rain down from above. We figured we both knew who was responsible for the rocks: the same creatures who had made the prints the day before. Like rowdy youngsters, they seemed upset that someone had invaded their playground.

I thought back to Emily's description of the young Skookum in her yard and the big one standing guard. We had found one large, vague print off to the side where an onlooker might have stood. In the days to come we referred to this place as the babysitting beach.

Late that night, loud whistles coming from the road awakened me. A growling sound outside our bedroom window followed. It prompted me to scoot closer to John.

The next morning I wasn't surprised to find that all the rabbit snacks on Youdi's trail had disappeared. Once again, the wrappings had been neatly opened and left nearby. This time they appeared to have been licked clean.

For the next few days, I stayed close to the phone, willing it to ring. It had been five days since I had dropped off the film for processing. Late one afternoon I got the call I'd been waiting for. I told John to open a can of soup for dinner if I wasn't back in time and drove like a mad woman to the drugstore in Puyallup.

I screeched to a halt just as the woman was flipping over the open sign. I talked my way in. She must have thought I was demented to want a packet of photos so badly. I tore open the envelope and rummaged through a series of posing children and faded sunsets before I caught my breath at what I saw.

There were five perfect photos of various prints. I couldn't believe how clear they had turned out. I could see the depth and every crack where their weight had split the sand around the edges. They showed up better than the actual prints had. These were the first pictures I had taken since I was a girl and I doubted they would turn out.

I must have looked really odd to the clerk. "Are you all right?" She said.

"Huh? Oh, yes, of course."

I started to walk to the door and she began to relax. The crazy lady was leaving and she could close up now. She followed me to the door.

"NO, NO!" I shouted. "I've got to show these to someone!"

She put her hands up in defense and backed away. I riffled through the photos again and handed her one. "Here, look. What do you think this is?"

There was a moment of silence while her brain adjusted to what her eyes were seeing, then her mouth dropped open and the hair stood up on her arms. "My God, this is a Bigfoot track, isn't it? Where did you find this?"

"Thanks," I said. "That's all I wanted to hear." I grabbed the photo and ran for the door.

She was still standing there as I hurried to my car and drove off.

The photos were proof: not for the world, but for ourselves. So many strange things had happened but none of them could be proven or explained. This was proof of at least one thing... there *had* been Skookum on that beach. No one who saw the photos would have any doubt what had made them.

When I got home, I had John sit down before I handed him the envelope. I went off to putter in the kitchen. I had rearranged the photos so the Bigfoot prints were on the bottom of the stack. I could hear him grumbling about his muddy camera as I worked. When he came to the first footprint photo, I heard nothing. He hurried into the kitchen.

"You took these?"

"Of course I took those. I told you last week."

"I know, but I didn't realize how real they'd look."

"They look real because they *are* real, remember?"

That was what I meant about proof for us. The photos made Skookum real: not only to John but also to me. Now, whenever I doubted anything that was going on, all I had to do was look at those pictures.

I called Youdi to tell her how well the photos had come out. We laughed when I described the drugstore lady's reaction. Then she became serious. "It's a good thing you were wise enough not to tell her where the pictures were taken. Skookum would be in big trouble if word got out. Every gun-toting *pasaiook* in the county would be camping there."

"You're right. I'd better make sure John keeps his mouth shut at work tomorrow."

John didn't like it but he understood why he couldn't say anything to his buddies.

As sleep claimed me that night, I realized Dream Walker's prophecies were coming true. Paul and his friends were coming to join us and I had held the future of Skookum in my hands today.

Youdi was amazed when she saw the photos. "I don't know of anyone who has photographed the tracks of so many young Skookum. Paul will be very pleased."

"He won't tell anyone where these were taken, will he?"

"No, we can trust Paul and whoever he brings here. He has already been here once before. Most of the famous researchers have been. There have been many sightings here in the past but nothing like our group has experienced. I just hope we can keep 'Bwana James' from finding out any more. I feel so stupid having called that man."

"It's okay, Youdi. What's done is done. I know how you felt when you called him. I *had* to show the photos to someone and even James has more experience than a drugstore lady."

Chapter Fourteen

See the creature stalking
While we speak!
Hush and hide the talking,
Cheek on cheek!

— Robert Browning
"A Woman's Last Word"

The next few weeks were rather mundane compared to what we were used to. There were still occasional factory noises and smells, but all other signs of activity were absent. Over the past few months so much had gone on that the area felt lifeless and vacant when nothing new happened.

During this downtime, I longed for my journeys with Dream Walker. Each night, I sat by the window in the living room hoping to at least see his campfire in the sky over the ridge. The autumn star and its accompanying lights had been absent for over a month.

Autumn and I took daily walks to the river surrounded by the beauty of spring. The Earth Maiden had outdone herself this year. The cheery faces of dogwood flowers smiled at us from just above eye level. Maidenhair ferns stroked our legs and bluebells nodded at our passing. Bleeding hearts and sea spray bloomed on Youdi's trail.

I checked the nests high in the rotting logs, but there were no signs they had been used. One morning I discovered a spider's web, shining with dew, spread across the lookout that afforded a view of our living room. The ducks and chickens became comfortable eating the buffet of bugs behind Youdi's cabin. This, to me, was a sure sign the Skookum weren't near.

One night there was a report on the news that a man had seen a Bigfoot in the Auburn area, about forty miles away. I never heard any follow-up.

At any other time in my life, I would have been grateful just to be living in a beautiful place like as this. Now it wasn't enough. Questions had been awakened in me and I needed answers. The waiting seemed more than I could bear at times. If Paul and his friends arrived during this lull, they would think we'd made it all up and leave. Even Youdi was absent. She was planting her garden in town. The entire valley felt like it was sleeping.

Finally, Youdi came out to spend a weekend at her cabin. John agreed to stay with the girls and Emily's son Greg, while Youdi, Emily, and I walked to the babysitting beach. Curt and Randy were at their house sleeping. As we trudged down the dusty road, my father's words from a recent phone conversation came to mind, "Count your blessings." I had complained to my parents about the fact that the valley was normal. They sounded relieved. Suddenly I felt ashamed of myself. Here I was with a healthy family, living in a paradise, and I was dissatisfied. Somehow in that moment I regained my perspective and began viewing my world through different eyes. The road ahead took on a brilliance I was sure it hadn't had a moment before. Trees were a greener green and I felt the sun warming my back.

When we reached the barricade, I noticed once more the lack of birdsong in the area. Emily and Youdi had been talking while we walked down the road, but now they spoke in muted tones, as if a listener were nearby. I realized then that my change of attitude had come not only from counting my blessings. My mind and body held their breath... a change was coming.

As we descended the goat trail, a large crevice in the cliff caught my eye. About ten feet above beach level, it was almost hidden by cascading huckleberry bushes. I could see a black hole behind the delicate green leaves. I climbed onto a nearby boulder and peered in. The small cave had the same moss-lined interior as the lookout spots on Youdi's path. The back of my neck prickled and I backed out quickly. It smelled like Skookum.

Emily wanted to see if the smell was what she remembered, so I summoned my remaining courage and, together, we climbed back up. She was quickly satisfied that, although faint, the smell was the same.

"I'll never forget that smell," she said.

"Have you ever been to the B&I store?"

Her smile told me she had. "It's similar, but not the same. I won't go there any more. I can't stand to see that poor gorilla. I want to set him free."

We hoisted Youdi up so she could see the cave. Then we climbed down to the beach. The sunny, sandy stretch was unmarked by prints of any kind. We made our way to the water and sat on a boulder to soak our feet in the icy cold water that came directly off the glaciers of Mt. Rainier.

In the distance we could see remnants of the railroad trestle. I had forgotten the camera. It seemed like Youdi never would get a picture of that trestle. A branch cracked across the river and I ducked. Youdi laughed.

John met me at the door when we got home. He gave me a letter with a California address I didn't recognize. It read:

> Dear Sali,
>
> Paul recently sent me a copy of your children's story, "My Secret Friend." I devoured it. What a truly exquisite piece. I must meet the lady who wrote and illustrated this triumph of children's lit. I'll make plans to come your way soon. Paul has told me all about you people up there. I can't wait to meet you.
>
> Your future friend,
>
> B. Ann Slate

"JOHN!" I yelled. "Do you know who sent this letter? It's B. Ann Slate, one of the authors of my favorite Bigfoot book. She said she's going to talk to her agent about helping me get my book published!"

John had an odd look on his face after he had read her letter.

"What's the matter?" I said. "She likes my book."

"I guess I'm feeling a little ashamed. I've always considered your writing and drawing just a hobby. Apparently I should have taken your talent more seriously. This lady certainly does."

From that day on, John had a different attitude towards my efforts. If nothing else ever came of Bobbie Slate's letter, I had her to thank for that.

I was awakened later that night by heavy footsteps outside our bedroom window. I tried to wake John, but he slept on. The CB had finally died, so I lay there alone, listening as deep growls and the night birds followed. The valley was coming awake again.

When I went to let the chickens out one morning, their gate was open. This surprised me because John had built the latch so the entire gate had to be lifted up to open or shut it. The wind or small predators couldn't accidentally open it. I was sure I hadn't left the gate open when I put the chickens to bed the night before. Then the wind shifted in my direction... Skookum.

When I opened the door to the chicken yard and scattered corn, any doubt I might have had vanished. The chickens refused to come out. They cowered in their nest boxes, shaking.

The ducks were absent as well. Usually they came running to greet me with their new batch of babies.

I went to check on the rabbits. They cowered in their cages, and I noticed the heavy wire was bent in several places. One of the large does lay dead in her cage. I could find no marks or blood on her, so I assumed she had died of fright. I ran to get John.

He butchered the dead rabbit. Since we weren't sure what she had died from, we decided not to eat her. I divided the meat into bait packets and put it in the freezer. John decided he would butcher the remaining rabbits. He had been considering this for some time because the two older girls refused to eat the meat. Raising rabbits had become more hassle than it was worth, he said.

I took two of the bait packets over to Youdi's trail and came home to cut up the remaining meat and tan my hides. My thoughts went to Dream Walker, as they often did. Since the night I'd seen the braves bring down the elk in the forest, I never forgot to thank each animal for giving its life. Whether it was a pork chop from the grocery store or a rabbit from our own hutches, I gave silent thanks.

That evening, when I was saying good night to the girls, I heard loud thumping out back. I shined the flashlight toward the chicken coop, but could see nothing. Screams echoed through the canyon all during the night. The next morning when I went out to feed the chickens the gate was standing open again. I fed the hens inside. There was still no sign of the ducks. I hoped they weren't stacked up somewhere like cordwood. As I turned to go back to the cabin, I noticed that the rabbit hutches were upended. I assumed John had done this after butchering yesterday.

I was in the kitchen fixing breakfast when I heard a commotion out back. John's excited voice called my name. "Sal, Sal, come out here. Come see what they've done."

I ran to where John was standing. I hadn't noticed earlier, but the hutches were some distance from where they usually were. John was wiping sweat from his face with a handkerchief.

"Boy, are those suckers strong," he said. I guessed whom he meant. "These hutches have been dragged at least twenty feet; see the marks in the dirt? Then they stood them on end. But, look what they did back here."

We walked to the other side of the massive cages. I looked, in awe, at the splintered wood and bent wire. Two by six boards were ripped loose and sixteen-penny nails gleamed in the sunlight. The heavy steel wire was crumpled. John's eyes bugged,

"Do you have any idea how much strength it took to destroy that cage? I'd have a hard time doing any of that with a crowbar."

"I noticed earlier that the hutches were on end, but I thought you must have done it after you hosed them out."

"No way. It would take four of me to scoot those hutches even a couple of feet. I'm not so sure I want those Skookum coming around after all. I know you claim they're gentle, but what if one of them gets mad? I'm gonna load my shotgun, just in case."

"Oh John, no. Skookum have never been known to hurt anyone, unless that person was the aggressor. I don't want a loaded gun in the house."

"Tough. After seeing this, I'm keeping the gun by the bed. I'll make sure the girls know not to mess with it."

I felt sick as I walked out to pick up the mail. Dream Walker had warned me about pasaiooks with guns. I remembered the Skookum hiding in the mist and the sound of dogs in the distance. In my mind I smelled the scent of dead dogs littering the forest floor and saw the wounded giant limping off into the trees. I snapped back to reality when a car whizzed by. It wasn't a good idea to daydream in the middle of the road. In my hand was another letter from Bobbie Ann Slate. Over the past few weeks I had finished another children's book titled, "Crazy Lou." I had sent Bobbie a copy. I opened her letter and read as I walked.

> Dear Sali,
>
> Received your story today. I don't know how you do it. "Crazy Lou" is superb. We are kindred spirits. Paul and I are working together on a book that has similar

thoughts. He says they will be in your area in a few days. I wish I could stow away in someone's baggage, but that's not possible right now.

I hope I've not overstepped my bounds, but I've sent copies of both your children's stories to my agent, Martin Singer, in New York. I'll let you know what he says as soon as I hear.

Love to all there,

Bobbie Slate

I sat at the kitchen table, stunned. It had long been my dream to be a published writer and illustrator of children's books. I had heard how difficult it was to get published. It seemed with Bobbies help, it could happen. I could hardly wait to thank Paul for sending the first book to Bobbie. I knew Paul was an author as well but I hadn't realized they were working on a book together.

When I looked out the back window later that night, the autumn star hung over the ridge. I hoped it would still be there when our visitors arrived. Chattering and night birds woke me at 3:00 a.m. John's gun was propped against the wall on his side of the bed. I hesitated to wake him. I felt like I was sleeping with the enemy again.

I found the bait gone when I checked Youdi's path in the morning. I was surprised to find the paper wrappings torn into tiny pieces and stacked neatly. It was as if the Skookum were trying to show us we were dealing with intelligent creatures.

The chicken yard gate was still latched. The hens came warily out of their coop when I called. Then the ducks came quacking up the trail from the woods.

Youdi arrived later that day to spend the weekend. We had an appointment to speak with an elderly man named Clarence in town that afternoon, but first I wanted to show her the piles of paper. She picked up some of the pieces and put them into one of her leather pouches. "Paul will be pleased with these," she said.

Youdi's eyes grew huge when I showed her the demolished hutches and told her of John's loaded gun. "I hope he has more sense than most *pasaiooks*."

"So do I."

We drove to town in silence.

Clarence, the man we were going to see, had lived most of his eighty-three years in the area. Several people had mentioned his name as a person to talk to about the plane crash. No one ever said so, but I got the feeling he had been there that day.

Until recently, we hadn't been able to find out where Clarence lived or his phone number. No one seemed willing to tell us. It amazed me that people were still reluctant to discuss anything about the day of the plane crash after twenty years. Finally a man at the feed store gave us Clarence's phone number, but only if we told no one where we had gotten it. We called Clarence and he agreed to meet with us in his home. I had mentioned Bigfoot, but not the plane crash.

The small house looked deserted. All the curtains were pulled shut and the lawn wasn't mowed. When we knocked, it took several minutes before a tiny, stooped man leaning on an ornately carved cane opened the door. His eyes lit up when we introduced ourselves and told him why we had come. He hurried us inside.

We were seated at his dining room table and then he hobbled to a glass-fronted bookcase where he retrieved a huge atlas and a manila envelope. I rushed to help him. He allowed me to carry the atlas, but batted my hand away when I reached for the envelope. "No one touches this but me," he said.

When we reached the table, he opened the book to a map of Tibet. Youdi and I looked at each other with questioning eyes.

"After the big one," Clarence began, looking back and forth at us. "World War II, you ninnies... anyhow, back in those days I traveled extensively through Tibet and the neighboring countries. Sometimes I hitched a ride on a cart and sometimes I walked. I saw things most folks never see.

"One day, I arrived at a remote village just about sunset. High on a nearby mountain I could see this huge fortress that looked like it had been carved from the rock it sat on. Being interested in unusual sights, I asked a villager what it was. Language was a problem but I knew signs and a bit of the local tongue. He said the place was a monastery but I couldn't make him understand that I wanted directions to the trail so I could climb up. Eventually he made it known to me that there was no trail.

"When I laughed and asked how they got up there, he said if I would go to a certain spot at the base of the mountain at sunrise I would understand.

"For three days I rose in the dark and journeyed to the site he had described. Each day, although I witnessed a glorious sunrise, I returned to the village none the wiser.

"On the final morning of my stay, the sun was just peeking over a V between two peaks when something blocked it from view. I put on my dark glasses to remove the glare and was stunned to see a man in yellow robes floating to earth in a cross-legged position. When he came in contact with the ground he unfolded himself, stood up, and walked away.

"When he had gone I crept to the spot where he had touched down. A hand-embroidered mat lay on the ground. A small bit of its corner had been torn loose. I picked it up and put it in my pocket.

"That night I walked back to the spot hoping to see the fellow ascend but I must have been too late. I walked back to town in the dark. The next morning I left the village for other parts but I've never forgotten the sight of that robed man floating to earth."

Youdi and I were spellbound as Clarence opened the envelope and poured out its contents on the table. Among some foreign-looking train schedules and paper money was a piece of reed matting.

"You are the only people I've ever shown this to," Clarence said, touching the scrap reverently. "Now you know how the Bigfoot do it."

"Do what?" We both said.

"*Lung gum pa...* levitation. Now you know how they disappear. My buddy saw one when he was hunting once. He said one minute it was there, the next it was gone. All that was left was that God-awful smell."

All was silent in the stuffy, overheated room while we tried to think of something to say. Finally, Youdi spoke up, "That was a wonderful story and it certainly answers that question, but we're also interested in another mystery or two. We were told a meteor came to earth here in the 1950s and around the same time an Air Force plane crashed after colliding with a UFO."

Clarence's expression became wary. He got up and hobbled to the window, opening the curtain a crack and peering out. "You'd better be careful who you ask about that plane. You'll have strange men turning up on your doorstep. All I will say is that the two sights are in walking distance of each other."

"Do you know what hit the plane?" I asked.

"I can't rightly say but I heard it was something orange. Now let's change the subject. I'm an old man and I'd like to enjoy the time I have left.'"

"Can we talk about the meteor?" Youdi said.

"Oh sure, that caused quite a stir around here. After a while, someone told me the university sent out a geological team to test it. According to what I heard, they drilled down and took samples. What they brought up was almost pure iron. Now, I'm getting tired. You ladies will have to excuse me."

We thanked Clarence and gave him our phone numbers in case he wanted to tell us anything else.

On the way back, Youdi was silent for several miles. Then she said what I was thinking, too, "That was a strange conversation. I never expected to hear a story about Tibet."

"No, but you must admit he has a point."

"I suppose he does. That old man is still afraid to talk about the plane crash after all these years. Did you see his expression when I asked about it?"

“Yeah, he acted like someone had his living room bugged. I wonder what he meant about strange men on the doorstep.”

“I’ve read about something called ‘men in black’. I wonder if that’s what he was referring to,” Youdi said, staring off into space.

When I opened my door, the phone was ringing. It was Clarence. “After you ladies left I went to put away my mementos and the entire envelope was missing. You didn’t take my things, did you?”

I assured him we hadn’t and hung up. I thought he had probably misplaced the envelope but his accusation bothered me. I knew what to do when something was missing. My mother had taught me long ago. I sat quietly at the kitchen table and opened my thoughts... the answer came to me in an instant, as it often did. I called Clarence back. “This is Sal; you called about your missing envelope? I believe if you’ll look in the atlas under the map of Tibet, you’ll find it.”

“Hold on a minute,” he said. I could hear Clarence making his way to the bookcase and back. “I’ll be damned. How’d you do that?”

I smiled as I answered. “I guess I had help from someone higher up.”

I could hear Clarence chuckling as I hung up.

Chapter Fifteen

With step as soft as wind it passed
O'er the heads of men — so fast
That they knew the presence there,
And looked — but all was empty air.

— Percy Bysshe Shelly
"The Mask of Anarchy"

We had been waiting for this trip to the meteor site for months. Everyone was up early. I was packing a picnic hamper when I heard a soft knock on the door: Emily stood there with an odd look on her face and a strange story to tell.

She and Curt had been sitting on their couch the night before, when he let out a loud yelp and glared at her. He jumped up, accusing her of burning him with her cigarette. She hadn't even been smoking. They both noticed the same smell of heat we had all smelled in the woods. When Curt rolled up his shirtsleeve, he had a red patch the size of a quarter on his forearm. The fabric of his shirt wasn't damaged.

He told Emily of a similar incident a couple of nights earlier when he'd been in the bathroom, sitting on the toilet with the door shut. He showed her a reddish patch on his left calf. Both spots were the size of the small lights we had seen flickering through the forest.

Both Curt and Emily were terrified that these burns had occurred while they were inside. It shook their already fragile sense of security. As with the electrical oddities in our cabin, the events were frightening because they occurred within our "safe zone." When home becomes a part of the mystery, there's no place left to hide.

Emily had decided her family would stay home from the outing that day. John declined as well, saying he had too much work to do at home. Krista wasn't interested because there were no children her age in the group. Youdi, Amber, Autumn, and I left to join up with Pete and Janet's family at their house.

The day was windless and bright, with only a few clouds casting great shadows on the land below. The road was so bad we all had to cram into Pete's jeep for the ride to the crater. It was a tight fit, but we managed. After a bone-jarring climb up a rutted dirt road, we emerged from the trees three miles later to see a football-sized field atop the ridge.

I thought, "This is how an eagle feels." Virgin forest of old growth trees stretched as far as I could see. Here and there, tucked into pockets between undulating hills, were the matchbox homes of the area's few residents. Upriver, and to the west, lay the tiny town of Orting. The river snaked through the canyon far below. I could make out bits of rooflines where our string of cabins nestled beneath the tall trees. To the east, above it all, rose the snow-capped peak of Mt. Rainier, home of Skookum.

For several minutes we stood frozen in place by the grandeur of the spectacle before us. Even the children gaped in awe at more of the world than they had ever seen at one time. Then, as if a school bell had rung, children scattered in every direction.

"Hey, you kids," Pete yelled. "Stay away from that cliff. Come on over here. We're going to see the crater."

The crater itself was as large as a baseball diamond, and about seventy-five feet deep. I had expected a large hole, but the vastness of the crater was astounding. On all sides, nothing grew but spindly wild rose bushes and deformed sallal shrubs for at least two hundred feet. The earth had a reddish brown, baked appearance. I could see where years of motorcycle riders had made deep ruts down its sides.

"Back in the sixties, when I was a kid, this hole was twice this deep," Pete said. "My dad used to bring us up here to ride an old Harley he had. Back then, only the older guys, the daredevils, had guts enough to ride down into the crater. In those days you could still see how the trees around the edge were burnt and stunted. The dirt was still black where the meteor went in. It took a lot of years before anything grew back."

The whole area had an odd feel to it, windswept and isolated, like being on the edge of the world. I could still see evidence of the meteor strike twenty-five years before.

I scanned the surrounding forest and saw a slim break in the trees not far off. Pete and Janet agreed to watch the kids while Youdi and I explored.

The narrow path ended at another large clearing. The brush and trees here were no more than twenty years old. Scattered on the ground were the blackened remains of their elders. This and the meteor clearing were the only two breaks in an otherwise impenetrable stand of old growth forest. I didn't need to see any traces of airplane debris to know this was the place Clarence told us about. We ate our lunch at the crash site.

The next two days were almost unbearable. Paul, Toby, and their wives were driving up. Several times a day I imagined where they might be. I could feel them getting closer. I spent most of those two days cooking ahead so I could be free for the adventures to come.

Then a Suburban came to a stop in our driveway. Youdi's car pulled in behind it. Bodies erupted from every door. Hugs and greetings were exchanged.

Paul didn't look anything like I had expected. He was a short, swarthy type with huge, dark eyes. His wife, Hilda was a dark, quiet woman who was dwarfed by her husband's dynamic personality and authoritative voice. Toby looked more like I'd expected Paul to. He was tall, with brown hair worn in a ponytail at his neck. His eyes had an ethereal quality and looked deep into mine when he said hello.

His wife, Laura, was an outgoing, likeable woman with long brown hair tinged blonde from the sun.

After the waters of arrival had calmed, Paul and Youdi left to get Emily and her boys. The rest of us trooped inside.

The next few days were a blur of excursions and conversations around the campfire or my kitchen table. The visitors had set up camp on Youdi's ten acres down the road. They reasoned that as a halfway point between the babysitting beach and our dwellings it would upset activity in the area as little as possible.

Screams echoed through the canyon their first night. I wondered what they were thinking as I lay in bed listening.

The footprint photos overwhelmed Paul and Toby. I'd had copies made and gave them each a set.

I was surprised when John and Toby hit it off right away. John had always been so set against anything remotely connected with psychic phenomena, but he was fascinated by a series of topographical maps of our area that Toby had brought along. Together they spent hours going over these maps while the rest of us walked the woods.

One day, I listened to Toby and John discuss a theory of Toby's concerning vortexes. "I've triangulated three of the hot spots in the continental United States where an extraordinary amount of both Bigfoot and UFO sightings have occurred over the years," Toby said. "The Bermuda triangle and the eastern part of Florida are, for obvious reasons, one area. Apart from being part of a triangle in its own right, the east coast of Florida, alone, has had an inordinate share of activity of both types. The same holds true for parts of Pennsylvania. This area falls into the high activity category, as well. In all three areas, heavy mining has taken place at some time in the past: mineral deposits seem to correspond with UFO activity. All three areas have hundreds of miles of subterranean caverns. Pennsylvania is a coal-producing region, just like here. Florida produces limestone, phosphates, and Fuller's Earth.

"I did a reading on all three places recently and discovered a high iron content may have a bearing on these paranormal activities as well. Each of these areas may be a vortex. Do you know if there are any iron deposits in this area, John? I believe all this may have something to do with the magnetic properties of iron."

"Not that I know of, but it should be easy to check out. There should be mining records at the Tacoma courthouse, If not, I know a few people around we could ask."

I interrupted. "There's a huge chunk of iron very near here. The meteor."

Both faces turned in my direction. Toby's was eager, John's disbelieving. "How could you possibly know anything about mineral deposits around here?" He sneered.

"Because I've been researching that huge meteor that hit here back in the 1950s. The University of Washington took samples and found it was almost pure iron. You could have come along the other day when we went up to see the meteor site and where the plane crashed, John, but you said you were too busy."

"I'm not too busy," Toby said. "Tell me."

While John pouted, I explained what I knew about both events, then I showed Toby the account of the UFO/plane crash in the old Frank Edwards book. He was excited. "I'll research this more when I get home, but in the meantime could you take me up to see those sites?"

"Sure, we can go first thing tomorrow."

John wasn't happy. He had to work the next day.

I called Youdi to see if she wanted to come along but she had to take Bud to physical therapy for his burns. She sounded odd. When I questioned her, she said she was having some problems at home, but didn't go into details. I was worried, but didn't feel I should pry.

The next morning it was pouring rain. After I explained the treacherous condition of the road, even in dry weather, Paul decided they had better not risk the trip in their car. No one went up the ridge. The whole group spent the day packing for the trip home the following day.

Youdi called later that evening. I had never heard her so rattled. "A lot of really weird things have been going on here. I didn't know what to make of them, so I haven't said anything, but I need to tell someone. I don't like what's happening.

"A couple of nights ago, our TV started acting funny. Both the picture and sound kept cutting out. I looked all around outside to see if I could find anything that could be causing it, but I couldn't see anything obvious, like a neighbor's car or something. This happened several times. Finally, I thought I'd try something. I went to the bedroom and opened the window. I sent out loving thoughts, saying that I did want to be contacted, but in some other way. Instantly, the disturbances stopped and the phone rang.

"My daughter, Tina, came to find me, saying an odd sounding man was asking to speak to me. She said he wouldn't give his name and his voice sounded metallic. When I answered, the line was open for several minutes, but no one spoke. Finally, I hung up.

"The next morning I answered the door and two men stood there. They wore black suits that looked new and they both spoke in a monotone. They said they were selling encyclopedias; would I be interested? When I said yes, they looked at each other like that was the wrong answer. They had no samples and said they would go back to their car and get some. They walked down the street and never came back."

"That's pretty strange, Youdi."

"It gets weirder. I happened to glance at their feet as they left. They were barefoot and dirty."

"Barefoot?"

"Yes. New suits and barefoot. It looked like they had walked a very long way."

"Wow."

"I'm not done yet. This morning I took Bud to the hospital for his treatment. I always bring a book and wait in the car. Usually I read, or watch the busy street and the people. Today there were no cars or people, until this shiny black car came driving by so slow it was almost parked. It was some make of sedan from the early 1950s.

"The window was down and the man driving had his arm resting on the door. He was funny looking... long face, pointed chin, and dark hair. I couldn't see his eyes because he seemed determined not to look in my direction. I had the funny feeling that I had met him before.

"I tried to read my book, but I couldn't. When I looked up again, the car had stopped in the middle of the otherwise empty street. The man was leaning out of his window pointing a camera with a long lens at me. At first I thought he must be taking pictures of the hospital, then I realized the camera was aimed too low. He was taking pictures of me. When he saw that I had noticed him, he drove on.

"I was getting really uncomfortable by then. There was still no one else either walking or driving on the street. Again, I tried to read, telling myself I was being paranoid. Then I got a creepy feeling. I looked up and there he was... except this time his car was going in the opposite direction. He drove by looking straight ahead. I watched as he drove out of sight. About a minute later all the usual traffic and people returned to the street.

"Then tonight the TV went crazy again. I had to turn it off, it got so bad. The thought came to me that if I looked out the bedroom window I would see why.

"It was the autumn star, Sal. I called Bud and we both watched it for about twenty minutes. It moved slowly across the sky in the direction of the river then it just vanished. When I turned on the TV again, it worked fine."

"I wonder if all this has anything to do with our talking to Clarence? Remember his warning about the men on your doorstep? I'll call him in the morning."

At 9:00 a.m., I dialed Clarence's phone number. It rang and rang. Finally a recording came on, "This number is no longer in service."

The gang from California arrived as I was hanging up and I became lost in a fog of good-byes. They said they would stop to say goodbye to Youdi when they went through town. As I sat in the vacuum their leaving had created, I thought back to something ominous Toby had said as he hugged me goodbye. "You told me about an old man you and Youdi had questioned about that plane crash." I nodded. "Be careful with your questions. The men in black have a long memory."

My arms prickled and I thought of Clarence and Youdi. I grabbed up Autumn and we drove to town on the pretext of getting some milk. As I drove by the street leading to Clarence's house, I saw the spookiest thing: A spotless 1950s black car was parked across the street from his house. There was a man just sitting in the driver's seat. On the newly mowed lawn in front of Clarence's house was a for sale sign. It had not been there before.

I kept driving.

When I reached home, I called Youdi. No one answered. After several tries, one of her children answered. No one had seen her all day and there was no note where she always left one. They were worried. I spent a nervous day waiting.

Finally, she called late that night, "Cliff said you called."

"Yeah, are you okay?"

"I'm fine. No men in black." Her laugh sounded strained. "Bud and I went out to dinner. No one followed us."

"That's because I saw the car you told me about parked across from Clarence's house. He didn't answer his phone and there's a for sale sign on the lawn. His phone has been disconnected, Youdi."

Silence.

"Youdi... are you there?"

"Yes. I don't like this. From now on let's stick to asking questions about Skookum. I've been doing some reading and it seems these men in black play hardball."

"I'm with you."

The next time I drove by Clarence's house there were new curtains in the windows and children playing in the yard. No black car was parked across the street. We never heard from Clarence again.

Chapter Sixteen

To seek thee did I often rove
Through woods and on the green;
And thou wert still a hope, a love —
Still long'd for, never seen!

— William Wordsworth
"To the Cuckoo"

Toward the middle of June Youdi traveled to Bluff Creek, California to meet up with Paul and Toby again. Her son Mic went along to keep her company. They camped near the spot where Roger Patterson had shot the famous film.

With Youdi gone, the days at the river seemed long and lazy but our nights were full of the now familiar whistles, screams, and lights above the ridge. Then one night, the bird sounds and the vibrations of the waterbed awakened me as heavy footsteps thundered by the side of the cabin.

By the time John awoke and grabbed his gun, the footsteps had already gone by. I could hear the Skookum disappearing into the distance by the river.

The next morning, the gate to the chicken house was open again. When I talked to Emily later that morning, she said she had heard nothing.

Youdi was gone for a week then she had to catch up at home before she could come to the river. Finally on little Greg's birthday, July 2nd, Youdi came out for his party. I had really missed her. I'd grown so accustomed to having her in my life I'd forgotten how lonely it was before I met her.

I was at home making cookies for the party when Youdi knocked on the back door. I grinned when I saw the familiar round face I knew so well. "Hi, Youdi. I'm so glad to see you. Come on in and..."

"Be quiet and come with me."

I dropped what I was doing, no questions asked. I knew by her tone something was going on. Youdi led me to a spot about halfway down her path. "Listen," she whispered.

A hollow, rhythmic noise filled the air. It sounded like someone hitting a log with a baseball bat. Youdi pointed to a nearby tree. I watched in amazement as the tree vibrated in time with the sounds. The noise had the rhythms and pauses of Morse code, and it was quite loud.

We moved closer and put our hands on the trunk. The jarring vibrations came from inside the tree itself. Our eyes widened. Youdi spoke, "Stay here. I'm going to get Emily. She should be here, too. We've shared everything else."

Youdi returned with her daughter, and Emily added her hands to the tree. It continued its odd behavior for several minutes then Curt came to the head of the trail. It stopped instantly. There we were standing like a bunch of idiots hanging on to a tree.

"What the hell are you doing?" Curt asked.

We all talked at once, trying to explain what had been happening. Curt frowned, then put his hands on the tree. Nothing. But he did notice something that caused him to step back. The tree was covered with the same burn marks he bore on his body. We watched as he rolled up his sleeve to show us a fresh burn from the previous evening.

Curt told us later as we sat talking by the fire that when he saw those marks on the tree he was overcome by the same otherworldly sensation he had the night he and Emily had watched the Skookum from their window.

Curt left the path after he discovered the burns, but we three women stayed. As soon as he was out of sight, the sounds and vibrations began again. Over the next few hours the phenomena continued, except when one of the men was present. We discovered burn spots up to a height of about twelve feet. We wondered again if the tiny flickering lights caused these marks. Several nearby trees had the same burns.

"The talking tree," as it came to be known, was an alder, fourteen inches in diameter and about twenty-five feet tall. We counted nearly two hundred of the small burns, which ranged in size from a quarter to a golf ball.

Throughout the day Curt, John, and Youdi's son, Cliff, performed various experiments in an effort to duplicate the sounds we had heard. Everything from a baseball bat to slapping hands on the trunk failed to produce similar results. John even beat on the lower portion of the trunk with a piece of heavy iron pipe. This made a similar sound and movement but with nowhere near the intensity of what we heard.

John insisted the tree was hollow and some animal had been digging beneath, amplifying the sound as it kicked the roots. The tree appeared neither hollow nor diseased. Above our heads, its canopy of healthy, green leaves covered the path.

In a final effort to solve the mystery, the men dug around the base of the tree to a depth of at least three feet. The only evidence of burrowing was theirs. After replacing the soil, they gave up and left. We girls were about to follow when the noises began again. They continued for another half hour then stopped. I checked off and on for several days, but the sounds and vibrations did not return.

That night I awoke to the familiar heavy treads outside our bedroom. John got up and ran to the living room window, but he said he saw nothing. I noticed his gun was no longer beside the bed. He must have thought better about shooting a Skookum. I was relieved.

Later that same night jabbering and giggles awakened me again. I tiptoed to the window and sat on the couch. The woods were riddled with tiny lights. I wondered how harmless they were. I jumped when the forest was lit by a blinding glare. For an instant I could see clear across to the ridge, then the woods were once again wrapped in darkness.

Youdi called the next morning. She'd seen James on TV the night before. He had been spouting on about his Bigfoot experience in the Seattle-Tacoma area and all the friends he'd made. During the interview, he showed footage from the Roger Patterson film. He also spoke at length about some friends of his outside of Orting who'd had a multiple sighting in their yard. He said his investigations now centered near the town of Roy, where it had been reported that a Bigfoot had torn the screen door off a farmhouse and caused other minor damage.

Youdi snorted, "If this is true, it is one of the rare times I've ever heard of Skookum being destructive. The only ones I know about are your rabbit cages, the report from Ape Canyon back in the 1930s, and the Bauman report. Roy is so close enough to Fort Lewis that I can see why Skookum might flip out now and then. I can hear the artillery and bombs from my house. Paul said he is going to call the TV station that ran James' interview and tell them what a conman James is, so no more unsuspecting people will call his hotline."

Before Youdi hung up, I told her about the tiny lights and the brilliant flash. Youdi said if I noticed any activity out by the river that night some of it might be human. Her kids Joe, Cliff and his wife, Mic and his girlfriend Laurie, and Emily were going to camp on the beach behind Curt and Emily's house.

There was a loud banging at my door. I could hear Esther yelling from where I stood in the kitchen. I ran to the door and let her in.

She looked like she was having a heart attack. "Esther, Esther... come in. What's the matter?"

"Oh Sarah, I'm so scared. Did you see that big flash of light out back last night? I wondered if a plane crashed or something. Black Jack damn near come unglued. He smelled something strange when I let him out. Instead a going out to pee, he ran back in the house and hid under my bed, yelping and whining."

"I don't think it was a plane crash, Esther. There wasn't any explosion. I'm not sure what happened, but everything seems all right today."

Esther's breathing slowed as she digested my words. Then she bolted from her chair and scurried out the door. "I can't take no chances, Sue. If the end is in sight, I'm gonna go have me some fun. Gotta get fixed up and get to town."

The last I saw of Esther she was waving at a carload of people as she hurried down the road in her chenille robe and furry slippers. She looked like something from the Lavern and Shirley show.

I recognized the car Esther had waved at. It belonged to Youdi's son, Mic. I could hear shouts of greeting as the passengers unloaded in Curt and Emily's driveway.

Later that day, the kids and I walked back to the river to join in the fun. The adults talked while the children waded in the water. Around dinnertime, the fog began rolling in, so the kids and I trailed up the path toward home. Sound didn't travel out there by the water when it was foggy. The fog followed the river like a white carpet being rolled out. In only a matter of minutes, the edges of things began to soften and blur as though an artist had muted the objects with a smudging of his thumb.

When we reached the cabin, I could hear nothing of the campers out back, but later I heard loud voices and car doors slamming from the direction of Curt and Emily's house. Then a car drove off in a hurry.

I don't know what woke me later, but when I tiptoed to the big window in the living room, I noticed the fog was gone and the moonlight was flooding the woods with cool, silver radiance. I held my breath as if I had knowledge of what was to come. A garbled, chirping noise came from the direction of Curt and Emily's. As I watched in awe, a large, dark shape disappeared down Youdi's path. I let out my breath in a soft whoosh and sat on the couch. My eyes went to the clock and I noticed it was 3:00 a.m.

The next morning Youdi called early. It seemed all her kids had camped in her living room in town. They had come in late, all talking at once. When they calmed down, her youngest son, Joey, told her what had happened. "He said that about dark it got very foggy. They realized that they hadn't collected any firewood, so everyone took off in different directions to gather some sticks. When they got back to camp, everyone said they'd heard odd noises, but each thought it was the others making them. As they built the fire, they heard screams from up river.

"Joey had pitched their tent by the water's edge. Before long, they heard the sound of something large being thrown in the river. Next came the sound of sloshing water, like someone walking in hip boots. They could feel something walking, but couldn't see ten feet away because of the fog. He said it was even hard to tell what direction the sounds were coming from. Then an awful stink filled the air.

"That was all it took... they ran for all they were worth. No one had remembered to bring a flashlight, so they fell down a lot on their way back to Curt and Emily's. He said he's never been so scared."

Youdi snorted. "So much for my chicken-livered Skookum hunters. I'll see you in a couple of days. I'm coming out to spend a week at the cabin. Then on Bud's birthday he will be out to join me. He has to work this week, so I'll be on my own until then."

Youdi called again the next night to ask if I would go over to Emily's to tell her that Curt would be home late because his car wouldn't start. Bud had gone to help him.

It was only 7:00 p.m. but again fog blanketed the forest in a gray shroud. It was eerily still on Youdi's path behind her cabin. Only the tapping of condensation falling from the trees broke the silence. I knew Emily's house was no more than a stone's throw away but it felt as if I were the only inhabitant of this ghostly place. Then, even the dripping ceased and the silence was absolute.

I stood frozen for a moment, stunned by the feeling of being encapsulated in time. Off to my right came the sound of heavy footsteps. I glanced toward the sound but I could see no more than two feet in any direction. The fog formed an impenetrable wall that surrounded me like a heavy quilt.

The footsteps hadn't sounded again, but I could feel someone near. "Who's there?" I called out, shining my light into the thick mist. It shone no more than a few feet. No one answered. "I must have imagined it," I thought, as I moved forward. The beam of light picked out the beaten path as I walked in the direction of Emily's.

Off to the right, at the edge of the halo of light, I saw the weathered boards of Youdi's cabin. With a sigh of relief I marked the halfway point of my journey. I had taken only a few steps when the footsteps came again... slow and heavy.

"Who's there?"

The footsteps ceased.

A chill that had nothing to do with the weather crawled up my spine. Then the sickly sweet odor I knew well permeated the fog. In that instant I realized that the light I'd been using only made me more visible in the fog. I flicked it off.

The darkness and footsteps came at me from what seemed like every direction. I knew that whoever or whatever was there would burst through the fog any second and block my way to safety. I did the only thing I could think of. I ran.

I knew if I lost the path, I was in trouble. When I stopped for a moment to get my bearings, the footsteps stopped, too. Then a fresh wave of stench hit and my reflexes took over. As I retched into the bushes, a high-pitched scream split the air. With the taste of panic and vomit in my mouth, I ran blindly into the fog. A moment later I ran smack into the side of Emily's house. I felt my way around to the front door and pounded on it.

Emily opened the door only a crack, as if she expected to find an axe murderer on the other side, and I shoved my way in.

"Oh Sal, thank God it's you."

Then she saw my expression.

"What's happened? You look awful. I smell Skookum. What's going on? Come in. Hurry." She slammed the door behind me.

"It's okay, Emily," I panted. "Your mom called with a message from Curt. The car won't start and your dad went to help him. I told Youdi I'd come tell you, but I didn't realize it was so foggy. Something was out there with me. I heard footsteps on the path. I guess we both know what it was."

A few minutes later, there was a loud knock on the door. We both jumped. When Emily opened the door, John was standing on her porch.

"I wondered where you went. Boy, does it stink out there," he said, rubbing his nose "Youdi called back to say Curt's on his way home. I thought you might like some company on the walk home. It's awfully foggy."

The walk home felt much safer.

Youdi was excited when she arrived the next day. "The most beautiful thing happened to me when I was driving by the fish hatchery. I felt the sensation of heat like we have been experiencing around here. The sky was overcast with patchy clouds. Up to my right was a small, black cloud with a perfect beam of light coming from the bottom. It was shining down behind a hill in the area of Wilkeson, the same direction where the light shows have been. I pulled to the side of the road and watched it for several minutes. My heart was pounding. Then I started out again, turning down our road. I could still see it, off to my left through the trees, until I got to Esther's house. Then I lost sight of it.

"Last night Bud and I saw something at home, too. We were sitting on the porch and we watched an orange light move slowly across the sky. Bud said it was an airplane but he didn't seem so sure when it vanished before his eyes after moving at a right angle straight up."

Youdi settled in for her stay next door. She spent her first evening at Curt and Emily's, going back to her cabin to sleep. The next morning she came over early to have coffee with me.

"We had a bit of excitement last night," she said. "Curt was in the bathroom getting ready for bed when Emily and I smelled the heat. We heard a loud yell from Curt then he came running out holding his pants up. He had an angry red circle burnt on his forearm next to an old scarred one. He told Emily he couldn't take anymore. They're going to find somewhere else to live."

Neither Youdi nor Emily had seen anything unusual in the house when Curt got burned, but I'd been looking into our mirrored wall about the same time and had seen the tiny lights flitting through the woods again. This time they'd been behind Youdi's cabin, on her path where the trees with the burn marks were. Just after that a loud rumbling shook the cabin, then stopped abruptly.

Laurie, Youdi's daughter-in-law told us later she'd had a vivid dream that same night. In her dream she'd fallen asleep beneath the talking tree and was awakened when a tiny man came walking down the path. He had a big head and large, slanted black eyes. He spoke to her but his lips didn't move. He explained his kind had been attempting to communicate with our group in various ways because they could tell we were friendly toward them. They just wanted us to know they were there. Laurie asked why they didn't just talk like he was doing now. The little man said there was a purpose to what was being done and it would come clear in the future if all went well. Then she woke up.

On Youdi's birthday, we arranged a special surprise for her.

Early in the afternoon Emily and I set up a party amongst the big logs on Youdi's path. When the pre-arranged time came, Emily led Youdi to the party. Everyone was there except me.

Suddenly the air was filled with a low, moaning whistle and a rhythmic tapping. Everyone went silent. Again came the moaning sound and the pounding noises... only closer. No one on the trail even blinked as the sounds came near. Children clung to their mothers. Mothers held their children tight. The sounds were almost upon them.

Shivers rippled through the waiting crowd on that hot July day. Then I stepped around a fallen log.

I wore my old mink coat that the kids called "kitty" and I blew on the neck of an empty wine jug. I dropped the stick I had been hitting logs with and yelled, "HAPPY BIRTHDAY." I could see both disappointment and relief pass across the assembled faces. Some people burst out laughing; others sat straight faced. Curt and Emily were the last to recover. They told me later my performance had been too real to be funny. Curt smiled, but it didn't reach his eyes.

Youdi was overwhelmed by her surprise. "I bet I'm the only person alive who has had Skookum wish them happy birthday," She said. "Thanks, you guys."

In late July Curt and Emily held a big bonfire and barbecue for their anniversary. All Youdi's children and their families were present for the occasion. Even her husband, Bud, had come along.

The party lasted late into the evening and the fire burned low when Youdi called out, “Look, it’s the autumn star! Look, Bud, up over the ridge.”

Everyone turned to face the river. We watched in awe as the big light changed colors... red, blue, and green, then back to white in rapid succession. Then it began to elongate until the middle was no thicker than a hair. It quickly resumed its original shape before smaller lights zigzagged up from the ridge and were consumed by it. We all covered our eyes when a brilliant flash lit the sky.

I watched Bud as the show ended. He appeared stunned, backing into a chair and sitting down hard. “What the hell was that?” he said.

“It’s the lights I’ve been telling you about, silly man,” Youdi answered.

No one was sleepy any more after that. We talked late into the night. Bud had become one of us. He could not deny what he had seen.

During the next week, several things occurred in rapid succession. Emily knocked on my door at 6:30 one morning. She said she’d been out for an early walk before Curt left for work. When she reached the river, the sun was just coming up and ribbons of mist hung in the canyon. She walked up river where the neighbors on the far side of her were framing in a new two-story house at the water’s edge. There was just enough light for her to see the scaffolding alongside the house closest to her. Playing on the bars were the young Skookum she had seen in her yard. From that distance, she said she could see plainly but couldn’t hear anything. They were climbing and swinging like a couple of kids on a jungle-gym playing tug-o-war with some object, but she couldn't tell what. The odd thing was that they moved in slow motion. She said she watched them for several minutes, creeping closer all the time, until they seemed to sense her presence and vanished. She never saw "Biggy" but she knew he was near.

Tears rolled down Emily's face as she sipped her coffee. Her eyes were troubled. "What's going on?" I asked.

"We're going to California later this month to visit Curt's parents. When we come back, we're moving. Curt found us a place in town. I don't want to leave, but he's my husband. I guess I'll have to."

"Oh Emily, I'm so sorry. It'll be empty here without you and the boys. Autumn will be crushed."

After Emily left, I felt like a great weight had descended upon me. Autumn and I took a walk to the river, but the beauty did not touch me that day. I had to tell my daughter her best friend was moving. I remembered Dream Walker's words and hoped this wasn't the beginning of the end.

I looked into the distance where I could see the shell of the new house. I wondered how the neighbors would react if I told them about the visitors they'd had earlier that morning.

Youdi and her son, Cliff, came out later that morning. Together with Emily, they had made plans to camp out in Emily's yard.

I slept the entire night without dreaming. Tapping on my bedroom window, Youdi awakened me just after first light. I made coffee while she told me what had happened during the night.

"I was just dropping off to sleep when I saw a dark shape dart into the trees not fifteen feet away. At the same time Cliff said, 'Did you see that, Mom?' Emily was already asleep. Cliff and I tried to stay awake to watch and listen, but we must have fallen asleep.

"About two-thirty, Cliff shook me awake. Heavy footsteps were clomping through the trees so close our sleeping bags were shaking. Then whistles shot back and forth and the night birds began singing. I wondered whose stupid idea it had been to sleep on the ground. I felt privileged to be in the midst of it, but at the same time, I hoped Skookum weren't clumsy. I hugged my sleeping bag close until I could see in the gray light of dawn.

"Emily told me last week she and Curt were awakened by the footsteps right outside their house. They were followed by a high-pitched child's voice saying, 'It's over there.' This was about midnight. Emily said she just forgot to tell anyone, but I think she's keeping things to herself for Curt's benefit... like if she doesn't tell anyone, nothing really happened. It might be a good thing that they're moving. Curt's acting strange lately."

Later that morning James called. He was on the defense before I could even speak. "Don't hang up on me," he said when I answered. "You'd better listen. This is the chance of a lifetime. I've got a reporter here from the *National Enquirer*. I've told him all about Curt and Emily's sighting, and he wants to meet all you people out there. We can be there in an hour."

I felt like the top of my head would blow off. "You had no right to do that! What does it take to get through to you? Unless you want to be shot, you'd better leave us alone. If you bring that reporter out here, I'll tell him what a phony and a liar you are, so tell him you made a big mistake. Now, LEAVE US ALONE!"

I hung up.

I was almost asleep that night when I heard heavy footsteps coming from the direction of Curt and Emily's. The waterbed began shaking and I smelled heat. I heard odd scratching noises coming from the next room, then the living room lights went on full blast. I tried to wake John, but couldn't. The hair on my body bristled like antennae. There was no way I was going in there alone. I hunkered into the covers to listen and must have fallen asleep. When I awoke, it was morning and the lights had turned themselves off.

When I asked Emily if she had heard the footsteps the night before, she appeared reluctant to answer. Finally, I got her to admit she'd heard them, but I could tell there was more she wasn't saying.

I was washing dishes that evening when I glanced over at Youdi's path. Mist was creeping through the trees like a gray carpet. At the back of her cabin was a darker gray object about three feet tall. It was shaped like a tombstone. Now and then it disappeared from sight as it seemed to float just off the ground. Then it moved slowly toward Curt and Emily's. I rushed outside, but it had gone.

It wasn't quite dark yet and I walked to Emily's house. She saw me standing outside and opened her door. Her eyes looked hollow. "What are you doing here, Sal? Is something wrong?"

As I explained what I'd seen, I watched Emily's face crumple. She sat down and sobbed. "I knew it, I just knew it," she said. "I saw that thing in our yard today, earlier. I didn't say anything because I didn't want to be the one to make something happen. I was afraid it was an omen that one of us was going to die. I don't like all this stuff anymore. I'm scared."

"Calm down. Just because you see something doesn't mean you have any power over whether something happens or not. Remember that I saw it, too. I'm going to go call your mom. Maybe she has some idea about what this all means."

I rushed home to call Youdi before it got too late. She was crying when she answered. "Oh Sal... I was going to call you. I just hung up from talking to Paul. He is devastated. Bobbie Slate died today."

Youdi's voice seemed to come from a long way off. I was gripped by a wave of nausea. I must have hung up because the phone rang again a moment later. I couldn't answer. All I could think was, how am I going to tell Emily? Emily and Curt were supposed to meet Bobbie and Paul in a few days when they went to California. Now she would feel responsible for Bobbie's death. I hadn't even told Youdi about the headstone Emily and I had seen.

I couldn't face Emily that night with my horrendous news. I crawled into bed and lay staring at the ceiling. Bobbie was dead. None of us had even gotten to meet her.

The whistles and screams that came later barely registered in my consciousness. I must have fallen asleep because when I opened my eyes the first rays of sunlight were warming the blanket. I dressed and slipped quietly out of the house, then down Youdi's path where I could walk without being seen.

Though Bobbie had never been here, she accompanied me on my solitary walk that morning. I told her of Youdi and Emily, even Dream Walker. I took her to all the places I loved so well. On that morning we became friends. When I could walk no more I went back, pausing at the corner of Youdi's cabin to bid Bobbie goodbye. I knew from that night on I would see her campfire in the sky.

Then I went next door to talk to Emily.

Youdi's car was already in the driveway. I felt a guilty relief that I did not have to be the one to tell Emily of Bobbie's death. I could hear Emily weeping as I drew near to the door. Youdi answered when I knocked. Emily was prone on the couch. Youdi came outside and closed the door.

"I took a long walk this morning. Bobbie's spirit came with me."

"I did the same. Just before dawn, I tossed flowers in the river for her. Let's go in and talk to Emily."

Emily was feeling somewhat better by the time I left. Youdi and her daughter meant so much to me. We were bound, not only by friendship, but also by the mysteries that surrounded us. Each would have been a bond by itself, but the combination formed a link so strong I doubted anything could separate us.

I found out the next morning the orange ball had been in Emily's yard during the night. She was awestruck. "It was beautiful. About the size of a basketball. All around it was a glow, like it was alive. It wasn't alone. Shortly after it cruised through the yard, I looked out again. The yard was lit up. I thought someone had driven in and I just hadn't heard them.

"At the end of our driveway was a bar of lights about five feet long. They were like the hunter's have on their trucks. When I opened the door to see if someone was here the thing took off down the road towards your house. I could see it clearly. There was no vehicle of any sort, just that weird bar of lights.

"Why do you suppose all this strange stuff is happening to us? Each one of us has had separate experiences, yet they all seem connected. I'd really like some answers. I'm afraid to stay here, but I don't want to move. I don't want to miss out when the answers begin to show up. I guess what I feel is frustrated. I keep asking, 'Why me, God?' "

"Don't worry, Emily. You won't be left out. It's not like you'll be leaving the country. Your mom doesn't live out here, but she's just as much a part of all this as anyone. Besides, you can always come out when she does."

Emily hesitated. "I don't know. I don't think Curt will want to come back here for any reason. He can't wait to move."

"Then come without him. You and your mom come and bring the boys. Autumn is going to miss Greg and Randy terribly. I haven't even told her you're leaving yet."

Emily hugged me tight. "Thanks, Sal. You make it easier to move on."

About noon I went out to get the mail. When I shuffled through the envelopes I stopped cold. There was a letter from Bobbie Slate, postmarked the day she died. My hands shook as I opened it, then my eyes filled as I read.

> Dear friend,
>
> Next week I get to meet Youdi's daughter and her family. Paul has arranged for all of us to spend the day together at Magic Mountain. Through knowing Emily I will be taking the first step toward being with all of you.

I feel as if we have been friends in other times. I don't even need to see you to love you. If you find you have company when you are walking alone in the woods, don't be surprised. I am already with you in spirit.

Your friend,

Bobbie

She had included a photograph of herself. I would treasure it always.

Chapter Seventeen

One impulse from a vernal wood
May teach you more of man,
Of moral evil and of good,
Than all the sages can.

Sweet is the lore which nature brings;
Our meddling intellect
Misshapes the beauteous forms of things —
We murder to dissect.

— *William Wordsworth*
"The Tables Turned"

A week later Emily and her family left for their vacation in California. They were not coming back to live at the river. All their things had already been moved to their new house in Tacoma, not far from Youdi.

Autumn was in mourning. She moped around the house like a sick dog. The two older girls would be starting school again soon and Autumn's best friend had moved. I made a point of taking her across the river to visit with Timmy whenever I could and I tried to interest her in cooking or gathering herbs with me, but it was no use. She needed to be with other children and have things to occupy her active mind. If only she could go to school, I thought. Her birthday was only a few days too late for me to register her in kindergarten, but because of those few days, I would not be allowed to enroll her until the next year.

One morning Autumn came into the kitchen with tears in her eyes.

"What's the matter, honey?" I asked.

"Didn't you tell me you think Skookum hibernate, Mom?"

"Yes I did."

"Well, is hibernation the same as death?"

I was floored. I answered Autumn's question and she seemed to feel better. But the fact that she had the ability to ask it told me she was ready to be in school.

I called the grammar school in town to see if there was any way they could enroll her this year even with her late birthday. The woman told me there was a series of tests for such cases, but they didn't recommend going to such extremes. It would be better if Autumn waited until the next year. She didn't know Autumn. We left for the school ten minutes later.

Autumn aced the tests.

When we left the school, we went shopping for school clothes. I hadn't seen Autumn that excited since the Skookum had taken her Dapper Dan.

I didn't realize how empty the days would be until after the bus had taken away all three girls that first day. Autumn would be home at lunchtime, but that was hours away. The fact that I had a whole morning to do whatever I wanted seemed like punishment. Even Emily wasn't around anymore.

The first few days I wandered the woods alone. The surrounding beauty escaped me until I began talking to Dream Walker in my mind. He didn't answer, but then he never really had. I knew in my heart he could still hear my thoughts. I wondered if he and Bobbie had met. I hoped so; it was a comforting thought.

Youdi came by one day about a week after Autumn started school. We planned a surprise outing. I arranged for Autumn to get off the bus at Janet's house and stay there until I picked her up later in the day. Youdi wouldn't tell me where we were going. When I asked, she talked about Skookum instead.

"Paul called last night. He and Toby have been working with another psychic. She's a teacher in the field. Her name is Tami. They both feel she's quite gifted. Paul said her vacation is coming up and she would like to spend it here with us. She is very interested in our research."

"Gee, that would be great, Youdi. I've had psychic abilities since I was a kid, but I've kept them to myself. Things like that frighten people. I would love to be able to hone whatever gifts I have to make them more useful. The thing I've always been able to do is know things about a person by holding some object of theirs. I found my ability quite by accident."

I was in an antique shop and I picked up a necklace. A great feeling of sadness overwhelmed me and I dropped the necklace onto the counter. When I spoke the name of the woman it had belonged to, the lady who owned the shop snapped to attention.

"Did you know Mary?" She said. "No, you couldn't have. She died over twenty years ago, and you're only a girl."

I couldn't explain how I knew the name of a dead woman I had never met, except that some of her essence remained in her property. The shop owner asked if I would hold the necklace again to see if I could feel anything else. I really didn't want to, because I hadn't liked what I'd felt the first time, but she looked so hopeful I didn't feel I could refuse.

I was taken to sit in a comfortable chair in the back room of the shop, and the owner left me alone after handing me the necklace.

Almost immediately, images came rushing into my mind's eye... a room with heavy old furniture... a tall, well dressed woman in her late forties humming an off-key tune. She was arranging flowers at a table by a window. Her back was to the door.

The edges of the picture darkened as a man entered the room. He stood silently for a moment, observing her. Then he whispered her name..."Mary."

She turned to smile at this much younger, slimy looking man, and the same necklace I was holding sparkled in a shaft of sunlight. The man embraced her, and whispered he loved her. I could feel his lies.

Then the scene shifted. The woman was alone in bed. Downstairs a dark figure entered through a window and went directly to a wall safe. The woman awakened and seemed to sense the intruder. She crept down the stairs and stood watching the man from the doorway. Even though he wore a mask, she called his name... "Gerald?"

His head came up and he turned, startled. Then he hurried toward the open window to escape. She followed him, pleading. "Why, Gerald, why? I would have given you anything."

"I know," he said, "but then I still would have had you." He grabbed her throat, and squeezed. I could see the life leave her body.

I found myself sitting, once again, in a chair in the back room of an antique shop. Tears streamed down my face, and I felt more tired than I ever had in my life. I had just witnessed a murder. I rested a few minutes, then went to find the owner. When I placed the necklace in her hand, I asked if the name Gerald meant anything to her.

"God yes," she said. "Gerald was Mary's husband. He was a slippery character, quite a bit younger than she was. We all tried to talk her out of marrying him, but I guess she was so flattered by the attentions of a younger man she couldn't see what he was like.

"The night she was killed Gerald swore he was home in bed with Mary the whole time. He went down to check when Mary heard noises. She must have followed him. A masked intruder knocked him out, and when he woke, he found Mary dead by his side. The police couldn't prove anything different, and they never found the intruder. This necklace was one of the few pieces that wasn't stolen. Mary had taken some of her jewelry to be cleaned that day. It was her favorite. Eventually it was returned to Gerald and he sold it after inheriting her estate. Her stolen jewelry was never found. I bought this necklace from the man Gerald sold it to."

"I saw Gerald kill your friend," I said. "I'm sorry. She seemed like a nice lady."

"I'm sorry too," she said. "But Mary's family will be grateful. Gerald died several years ago. He lived out his life in comfort on Mary's money. At least now her family will know the truth."

Youdi's eyes were wide when she glanced in my direction, but she said nothing as we turned into the driveway of a tidy, middle class home in Seattle. Our attention was directed elsewhere to a dark-haired man who had come out to greet us. I recognized him from his numerous appearances on TV.

Professor Grover Krantz first shook Youdi's hand, then mine. As head of anthropology at the University of Washington, he had a keen interest in Bigfoot research, even though that interest made him an outcast among his peers.

Professor Krantz led us to a side entrance and unlocked a basement door. The room we entered was a treasure chest of Bigfoot information. Poster-sized photos of various drawings, casts of footprints, and stacks of data on sightings filled the small space to overflowing.

I watched his eyes light up when we told him of some of the occurrences in our area. He didn't agree that Bigfoot and UFOs had a connection, but listened with interest anyway. His reaction to the mention of James was comical.

"Is that jerk still around? I'd have thought someone would have bagged and stuffed him by now."

Professor Krantz treated us to a private showing of the Patterson film that day. The female Skookum was breathtaking. Walking along a creek bed, her pendulous breasts were clearly visible.

On the ride home, I realized my attitude had improved. The outing and the fact that Tami would soon be arriving had lifted my spirits. I didn't even think about Youdi's lack of reaction to my story.

The next morning, I watched from Youdi's path as a truck unloaded its contents at Curt and Emily's house. A rough looking man and a big German shepherd went into the house after the truck left.

When I opened my door later, the dog was on the porch growling at me, its hackles raised. Then the man was there. He grabbed the dog by the collar and jerked it away. "Sorry," he said over his shoulder. "It won't happen again."

But it did.

That afternoon I heard Autumn's terrified scream coming from our front yard. The dog had her backed into the corner, ready to attack. The dog's owner grabbed its collar as it lunged for my daughter's face. Autumn cried as I held her tight. I was furious. "You keep that monster contained or I'll call someone to come get it," I screamed as he dragged the dog home again.

"So much for the new neighbor," I thought as I took Autumn inside. I never saw the man or the dog again unless it was in a car. I found out later in town that our new neighbor had recently been released from prison. I was glad he had decided to keep to himself.

I did my herb gathering far down river that year. It made me sad to see Emily and Curt's house with all the curtains shut.

The feel of fall was in the air the day I finished my gathering. The inside of our cabin looked like a Chinese apothecary as my herbs dried, but eventually everything was bagged and bottled for the months ahead.

Youdi didn't come out much during the last weeks of good weather. Her mother was in the hospital, plus she had canning to do. We managed to talk often on the phone, but it really wasn't the same.

Early one morning, my mom called to say they would be coming up for a visit. She asked where the nearest motel was. When I talked to Youdi later that day, she said they could sleep in her cabin. I didn't think my parents would agree because they were used to the comforts of city life, but they were thrilled.

Several days later, a big gray Cadillac pulled into our driveway. In it were two of the people I loved most in the world. I missed them terribly. My parents were wonderful, loving people. Good sports, too, I discovered. We unloaded their fancy luggage into Youdi's dark, rustic cabin and my mom set right to work sweeping and unpacking. This small box, with no running water or electricity, was to be their quarters for the next two weeks.

The following days were filled with excursions to all the places I had written to them about. No screams echoed through the canyon. No lights put on a show above the ridge. And no footsteps thundered by the cabin in the wee hours of the morning. The forest seemed to hold its breath.

I knew it wouldn't last long.

One morning, my dad came into the kitchen and rested his gentle hands on my shoulders. "Sal, I'd like to talk to you about all the odd things you've written to us about. Your mother and I have been rather concerned about your state of mind. It's fun to have fantasies, but we're worried this paranormal stuff is becoming an obsession with you."

As he talked, we walked to the living room. I sat on the corner of the couch and my dad stood by John's recliner. He continued, "Your mother and I feel that perhaps you have been reading something more into what are only everyday occurrences. Since we've been here, we've seen nothing unusual. We thought maybe if you got out more..."

As he sat in John's chair, the floor lamp went on over his head. "What the... what did that?"

I laughed. "Oh, that's just one of our everyday occurrences, Dad."

The overhead fixture chose that moment to come on bright; then as we watched, it dimmed and shut itself off. From the other room I could hear the washer filling. I ran to unplug it and turn the hose off at the wall. On my way back through the kitchen, I noticed that all four burners were red so I unplugged the range. No more was mentioned about my getting out.

My parents had been there about a week when Youdi finally broke loose to come meet them. They acted like they'd known each other forever.

Youdi invited my parents, John, and me to a lecture in Seattle the next evening. Dr. J. Allen Hyneck would be speaking. I called one of the teenage girls in town and she agreed to come home with the girls on the bus so we could leave early to have dinner on the way.

Dr. Hyneck's speech was interesting. He had been one of the experts hired to put together a government study called *Project Blue Book* in the 1950s. He had started out as a skeptic concerning UFOs, but he was soon an ardent believer. We had hoped to speak personally with him following the lecture, but his attitude during a question and answer period changed our minds. He was especially rude to one woman who was clearly upset by her experiences. After the lecture, Youdi followed the woman out and gave her our phone numbers if she wanted to talk to someone.

Later that night, I heard odd metallic noises coming from the living room and smelled heat. The ceiling fixture came on bright again. When I tried to wake John, I was unsuccessful. It was as if he was drugged. I finally pushed him to a sitting position but he held his arms straight up over his head.

At first I thought he was awake and joking around but, as his odd behavior continued, I realized it was no game. His eyes were open but he looked past me like he was hypnotized. He began speaking in a low voice that sounded nothing like his own. His words were chilling, "There's a leaf on top of it and a line runs to the middle of the earth."

I shook him. "John, what are you talking about?"

"Don't worry," he droned on. "It won't hurt you."

Then he fell over on the bed and started snoring. It took me a long time to get to sleep. The light in the living room remained on. I had such a creepy feeling; there was no way I was getting out of that bed. Every so often, I could hear the soft metallic clanking I had heard before.

The next morning when John came into the kitchen, I told him what he had done during the night. When I repeated the things he'd said, he looked at me like I was crazy. John said he didn't even remember dreaming. It was the first time I had ever heard John talk in his sleep.

I went for a short walk before my parents came over for breakfast. Halfway down the path to the river I heard musical notes, like scales, in a woman's clear voice. They were coming from the trees above my head.

The phone was ringing as I came in. It was Youdi saying she had just spoken to Tami. "You'll love her. She is so sweet. I feel like I have known her for years. Paul and Toby have filled her in on everything that has happened here, so she should be able to help us find some answers."

Tami was due to arrive in a couple of days. She planned to stay at Youdi's house in town for two days and then come out to stay with us. Krista and Amber had volunteered to double up so Tami could sleep in Amber's bed.

I was really looking forward to Tami's arrival. Paul had recently told Youdi about a series of classes in psychic development Tami had taught down south. I hoped to have the opportunity to hone my own skills and perhaps discover some new ones while she was here.

When my parents came in, my dad sat down in John's chair to read his paper. He reached for the switch to turn on the lamp, but the ceiling fixture came on. I heard him clearing his throat as he tried to turn that light off and the floor lamp on. When I went into the living room, I saw that he had given up. He was sitting on the edge of the couch reading by the light from the window.

I had to believe that these electrical malfunctions occurred for John's benefit. They were things he couldn't explain away or fix. I smiled as I plugged in the stove to heat water for coffee.

I was washing dishes when I noticed a heron standing in the duck pond. As I watched, it disappeared. All that remained was a shimmering patch of air, like heat waves in the summer. Then that too was gone. Autumn came in later with a heron feather she had found by the back steps. All these things were happening. Perhaps Tami could shed some light on these occurrences as well.

The next two days seemed to last forever. Then I looked out the door and Youdi's car was driving in. My parents had taken the girls for a walk, so I approached the car alone. I hugged Youdi and watched a tall, stunning woman with chestnut hair emerge from the passenger side. It was one of those moments when time stops.

Our eyes met with what seemed like instant recognition. Tami came around the car and grasped my hand in both of hers. A jolt of what felt like electricity shot up my arm to my solar plexus. "You're Sal," she said, in a husky voice. "I'd know you anywhere." I felt our souls touch in the moment that followed. It unnerved me and I struggled to maintain my composure. I knew then that Tami's presence here would be life changing. What I didn't see yet was that this was the beginning of the end.

"Uh... let's go inside and have coffee," I stammered.

Tami looked pleased with herself. Youdi appeared stunned at what had transpired. She must have felt it, too. I wondered if their meeting had been as powerful.

My right hand still tingled as we trooped into my cabin. I shook my head in an attempt to regain control as I began puttering in the kitchen. Tami talked nonstop, but Youdi was subdued and silent, her face a blank mask.

Since we three were alone in the house, Tami asked if we would be interested in a lesson in psychometry. She unclasped her necklace, handed it to me, and explained what to do. "Just say whatever you feel, even if it sounds silly to you."

She didn't even give me time to explain that I had done this many times before; I just hadn't known what it was called.

Tami wrote as I closed my eyes and spoke. At one point, I heard her gasp. She had tears on her face when I opened my eyes. "You've done readings before, haven't you?"

"My whole life. I never even tried to, it just happened. It used to scare people when I was little."

Tami handed me the paper she'd been holding. "Well, you're right on the money. No one's ever known the things you just told me about my father."

My hand shook as I read the disjointed words.

First word celery — no sedative — tingling in the neck — knees weak — feels good — am up above — liquor.

Below is farm — horse — gold color— buckskin — willow tree — nice place — country — 80s — 84°, nice weather. Someone Tami knows lives below. Father, gray hair and black. He has to get back to this place.

Airplanes — doesn't work on them. Doesn't believe in psychic. Drinks — too much liquor. Full moon — something will happen then — California, Simi Valley.

Sadness — great sadness.

Tami spoke from a distance as she explained that she had tried to warn her father not to fly his small plane that day. "He never made it to the farm," she said.

Next Youdi attempted to do a reading. She seemed reluctant, but Tami insisted that Youdi hold her hand, rather than using an object. She explained this was another method. Youdi looked uncomfortable, but closed her eyes and did as Tami said. Tami wrote with her other hand while Youdi spoke in a halting monotone. None of what she said made any sense to me. Then Youdi's eyes popped open. She jerked her hand from Tami's, grabbed the paper Tami had been writing on and bolted for the door. "I've got to go. I cannot do this anymore." Then she fled.

"Wait, Youdi." I called. But she was already gone.

"I wonder what that was all about." I said to Tami.

"Youdi has some personal issues to work on before she can let go of her conscious self. She's afraid of what will come out if she relaxes her control."

"That's crazy. What could Youdi have to be afraid of? She's the most together person I know."

The subject was dropped when my parents came in with the girls. But I thought about Youdi all day. She called late that afternoon to apologize for her abrupt departure. She said she had a lot of things on her mind. I told her I understood, but I didn't at all. There was a distance in Youdi's voice that had never been there before.

When I introduced John to Tami, they shook hands. He blushed like a schoolboy. I assumed it was because she was so pretty. (Looking back I'm pretty sure John got the same kind of shock as I did.) Several times during the evening, I saw him staring at her when he didn't think I could see him.

After my parents went to bed and the girls were asleep, Tami and I sat down to resume my training. John came over and asked if he could listen in. I was pleased because he had never shown interest in anything like this before.

During our discussion, John surprised me by asking some intelligent questions. He sat quietly while Tami explained the various types of psychic gifts, looking rather overwhelmed by the time she paused. Then he asked, "Does a person just have one or more of these gifts, or do they pick one and practice until they get it right?"

Tami smiled, then reached across the table to cover John's hand with her own. "Most of my students were young children when their gifts became apparent. You don't choose them. You're born with them. Some children have miserable childhoods because these gifts are so misunderstood by those around them. For instance, how would you react if one of your girls told you she had seen a creature most people believe is only a legend? Would you punish her for lying, or call her crazy?"

I watched as John squirmed in his chair. I wondered if he was thinking of Amber's sighting across the river or his own. "What does that have to do with psychic abilities?" he asked in a voice much softer than normal.

"Some researchers believe that Skookum repeatedly show themselves to humans they feel an affinity with. Usually it's women and children. In some cases the relationships have lasted many years... How did you feel after you had your sighting?"

I could see the blood drain from John's face. His mouth moved, but no words came out. Just then the phone rang and he leapt to answer it. Tami turned her attention to me.

"Saved by the bell," I thought.

Later when we were in bed, John informed me that he had decided to take some of his vacation days so he could spend the time with our company.

Chapter Eighteen

I, who can feign no image in my mind
Of that which has transformed me: I, whose
thought
Is like a ghost shrouded and folded up
In its own formless horror...
— Percy Bysshe Shelley
The Cenci

The next morning my parents took the girls out for breakfast at the local restaurant. We didn't go out to eat often, but this had become a yearly tradition for the girls and their grandparents. The girls referred to the restaurant as "The Breakfast Store."

Tami and I decided to walk to the babysitting beach. I was surprised when she emerged in an expensive pair of designer jeans, cashmere sweater, and new white tennis shoes. Her hair appeared freshly styled, and she smelled of Channel #5. I certainly felt like a country mouse in my hiking boots and flannel shirt, but I couldn't imagine sliding down a goat trail in her get-up.

"You'd better change into some old clothes. You'll ruin those."

"These are my old clothes," she said.

As we walked to the road, John's voice called out. "Can I come too?"

"Sure," Tami called back. "The more the merrier."

I would have preferred he stayed at home, but I didn't say so. I had several things I wanted to discuss privately with Tami. I couldn't seem to get her to myself. John began right off telling Tami one of his boring stories about work. She listened attentively. My mind wandered to our surroundings. The air was crisp with fall. A haze of smoke from the woodstoves hung over the valley. I smiled as I remembered the cook-fires in the village from my journeys with Dream Walker.

When I looked ahead John and Tami were almost out of sight. Her musical laughter came back to me on the breeze. I didn't catch up to them until we reached the barricade.

John went through the low hanging trees on the jeep trail first, holding back the heavy limbs so they wouldn't hit Tami. Those same limbs whacked me in the face as he sprinted ahead to hold the next one for her. At a wide place in the trail, I took the lead, navigating the goat trail with more bravado than I felt.

When I looked back, John was leading Tami with care along the narrow ledge. She cringed, looking as if she would fall to her death five feet below. John, properly attentive, grabbed Tami around her tiny waist and lifted her to the sand.

I did not like the green juices of jealousy that coursed through my system. Tami must have realized my feelings, because she left John's side and came to where I was standing. "I envy your courage. I was scared to death up there on that ledge. Thank God John came along."

I swallowed my reply and told her about the day Youdi and I had discovered the footprints. I was just about to tell her about the flying rocks when one hit me on the head. Tami squealed and we both ran to the safety of the cliff as more rocks plopped into the soft sand. When I looked around, Tami had scaled the goat trail with no help from anyone. John and I reached her side and I noticed that her hair stuck straight up, her sweater was ripped, and her shoes were covered in mud.

John tried to wedge himself between Tami and me on the way back but Tami bent to tie her shoe. When she straightened up, the two of us walked on together. Tami asked me about the first rock-throwing episode. John went on ahead while Tami and I spoke about that day on the beach. John had nothing to contribute to the conversation and seemed to want to reach home in a hurry. He had already passed the barricade when we reached it. I didn't see him again until we reached the cabin.

I felt ashamed of the awful thoughts I'd had earlier. My imagination had run away with me. After talking with Tami on the way back, I was sure again that John loved me and Tami was my friend. The feeling didn't last long.

Later that day my mom asked me to go into town with her to have lunch and do some shopping. Tami came in just as we were leaving. She had her notebook with her. She gave my mom an odd look. "I thought we could go over some of my lessons together, Sal. Are you busy?"

Tension filled the room. "I'm sorry, but we were just leaving. Maybe later tonight?"

"I see. Well, have a good time."

I noticed my mom didn't ask Tami to come along. Tami smiled when we left, but I could tell she wasn't happy at being excluded. I said goodbye to John in the yard. He was chopping wood. I glanced back as we drove off. Tami was standing by John feeling the muscle in his arm. My stomach knotted like a fist.

On the drive to town, both my mom and I were quiet. When she finally spoke, it wasn't what I'd expected to hear. "How long have you known that Tami person?"

"Not long. Why?"

"I don't like the way she looks at me. I don't think she likes the fact that your dad and I are here. She seemed upset that you were spending time with me today."

For some reason, I felt I had to defend Tami. "Don't be silly, Mom. She's just eager to teach me what she knows. She's very good at what she does."

"I'll bet she is. Just be careful, honey."

My parents had offered to take us all out for dinner the following night, so I splurged and bought a new outfit in town. It was late afternoon when my mom and I got home, so I hurried to start dinner. Tami sat at the table filing her nails while my mom and I cooked.

"I'd help you," she said, "but I'm useless in a kitchen."

Neither my mom nor I commented.

During dinner I noticed Tami watching my mother. After we ate, everyone but my mom and I went for a walk. We did the dishes and avoided talking about Tami.

The next morning Tami came out wearing a filmy pink nightie and those satin slippers with marabou feathers I'd seen only in the movies. John stumbled and dropped the armload of wood he was carrying. I was wearing a ten-year-old robe and a pair of John's thick socks.

Tami turned and batted her eyes at John. "Oh sorry, I didn't know John would be in here. Have you seen my jeans, Sal?"

"I washed them for you. I'll get them." I hurried to the dryer.

When I came back, Tami was standing in front of the full-length windows that led to the deck. The sun streaming in outlined her figure. John was on the floor, groping for the pieces of firewood like a blind man. His eyes were on the show. They both jumped when I cleared my throat. This time I knew my imagination had nothing to do with what I felt.

"Here are your pants, Tami."

"Oh, thanks." She came slithering over to me. Her eyes had the flat, hooded look of a female viper. "Something sure smells good. Sometimes I wish I were a housewife like you instead of having a career, but I'm no good at all when it comes to the homey things you do."

I tried to decide whether I'd just received a compliment or a put down. Somehow Tami's words made me feel positively bovine, like a comfortable old cow.

John was in the bedroom when I went to get dressed. I put on a pair of clean jeans and a comfortable shirt to go feed the chickens. He turned to look at me. "Did you ever think of buying some new clothes, or doing something with your hair?" He asked.

I knew whom I was being compared to. His remarks cut deep. "How about something in pink lace?" I shot back. "That would be just the thing for cooking and shoveling out the chicken coop. I'm sorry you're stuck with someone so plain, John. But look on the bright side... I can cook."

He left without another word.

That afternoon John's friend Greg showed up. When I introduced Tami, his eyes glazed over. From that moment on it was like they were glued together. John pouted for the rest of the day. I, on the other hand, was pleased.

My parents asked Greg and Tami to come along for dinner. It was a goodbye treat since they were leaving for home in the morning. We had reservations at an expensive place, for lobster. I paid special attention to my appearance, wearing my new, black pantsuit. Everyone told me how nice I looked except John.

After dinner, Tami and Greg left first in his truck. The rest of us rode in my parents' Cadillac. When we reached the fish hatchery, we scanned the sky for orange balls. Janet's daughter Shannon had seen one again recently.

The mouths of the coke ovens yawned wide like huge beasts at the beginning of our road. A bright light became visible behind us. We assumed it was Tami and Greg. The closer we got to home the closer the light came to the back of the car. It appeared Greg was playing a game of chicken with my dad; he was almost on our bumper.

I could tell my dad was nervous by the way he was driving. We took the steep turn into our driveway much too fast. We came to an abrupt halt and I sprang from the car, ready to light into Greg for his dangerous behavior. That's when I noticed his truck already parked off to the side. I realized it couldn't have been Greg because the light had gone on past. I walked to the road, but there was nothing there. The road was empty. The night was silent.

I thought back to the light I'd seen and realized it had only been one huge light, not two. The hair stood up on my neck when it dawned on me what could have been following us: the legendary phantom train Esther had told me about.

My parents said goodnight and walked to Youdi's cabin. Greg and Tami stayed inside the truck, with the windows fogged, until nearly midnight. John was already asleep when I heard Tami tiptoe in.

It was only 6:00 a.m. when I heard my mom come in. I was already in the kitchen making coffee. She looked like she hadn't slept at all. I went to her side, "Mom, what's wrong?"

"Can I talk to you outside, honey?" She looked in the direction of the girl's bedrooms. I saw fear in her eyes. I followed her outside where we huddled on the porch in the frosty air.

"I'm glad we're leaving today, I can't be around that girl anymore."

"Do you mean Tami?"

"Yes. She doesn't want me here."

"Mom, that's a bit much. I know she's kind of self-centered but..."

"It's a lot more than that," my mom interrupted. "She demands ALL the attention, and she wants me gone.

"I awoke in the middle of the night scared to death. Something was in the cabin with me. It was trying to control my mind. It took all my will to fight it. My whole body was tingling. I knew who it was. I was being told to leave in no uncertain terms. I also knew that if we didn't leave this morning as planned, something awful would happen to me.

"The only person I've ever known who has the power to enter another person's mind is your friend Tami. I've felt her venom since the first day she came. Haven't you seen how she looks at me?"

I nodded.

"When I was awake, trying to fight her, I heard the ducks quacking out back. Then I heard two loud whistles and heavy footsteps going toward your house. I smelled something burning, like the factory down the road at home. I don't know what it was. I didn't even have the lantern going. It was 3:00 a.m., and I was too terrified to move. I've never been so frightened.

"I love being here with you and your family but I'll be glad when your dad and I are on the road. That girl may have things you want to learn, but you'd better be careful about what she expects in return. You're too trusting. She's going to have you all to herself once we're gone. Protect what's yours."

I was stunned. My mom had never spoken like that about anyone before. My mom saying something like that really got my attention, at least for the moment. She had been worried about *my* fantasies two week before.

My mom hurried back to Youdi's cabin. When I opened the door to go inside my cabin, I almost hit Tami in the face. She'd been listening to everything my mom had said.

My parents left without eating breakfast. My family came outside to say goodbye. Tami didn't join us. When I turned to go back in, I saw Tami at the window. She had a pleased smile on her pretty face.

Chapter Nineteen

...I have watched
Thy shadow, and the darkness of thy steps,
And my heart ever gazes on the depth
Of thy deep mysteries.

— Percy Bysshe Shelley
"Alastor"

My parents had been gone only a couple of hours when I realized it was September 27th, my mom's birthday. In all the turmoil I had forgotten. In my mother's haste to leave, so had she. I hadn't even wished her happy birthday, much less had the celebration I had planned.

That same morning Youdi called. It was the first time I had heard from her since the day she had run from my house. She seemed more like her old self. She said an odd word kept coming to her. She asked me to write it down, fold the paper, and give it to Tami to see if she could do a reading from it. I did as she asked.

Tami held the folded paper in her clasped hands on the table. She closed her eyes and became still, then began to speak in a low voice:

"The word is Metro, no Meltro. I feel heat... hot... nervous... shaky. I want to start quacking... garbled talk. I see Youdi... reaching... stretching... reaching out... clenching her fists... reaching! Decision or understanding, something for Youdi. Some type of chemical or mineral... garbled talk."

Tami called Youdi when she was done with the reading to see why she could get no more. She nodded when she learned that Youdi had been doing automatic writing. Tami said the word "Meltro" was meant for Youdi to interpret, not her. Apparently, Youdi wasn't ready to do so yet.

Tami bent forward to look directly in my eyes. "Youdi has almost no natural abilities in psychic areas. She has to try so hard that it's amazing anything comes through. You would do much better to let her remain in her own little world while you and I go about solving the mysteries here. Youdi's weakness only makes it more difficult for us to succeed."

I was still reeling form Tami's words when her next statement stunned me. "It's better that your mother is gone, too. She's quite a disruptive influence, isn't she?"

I was on my feet, ready to defend my mother and Youdi when Autumn burst in the door.

"Hi, mom. What's for lunch?"

My hands shook as I fixed Autumn a sandwich, There was no way I could have eaten. My stomach was knotted like a fist and a fine sweat covered my body. I slumped into a corner of the couch and let the last hour replay through my mind.

I planned to talk to Tami outside while Autumn ate her lunch by the TV, but Tami had slipped out the back door by herself. Her escape seemed perfectly timed.

I sat staring out the window at the path that led to the river, but I saw nothing. Were the things I was learning from Tami worth the price? How could she dismiss Youdi so easily? Why had she driven my mother away?

If not for Youdi, I would know nothing about Skookum or the Indian ways that were now so precious to me. Would Dream Walker ever have made contact if I had not first started down the path where Youdi led me?

Youdi, Emily, and I were the three sides of a triangle. If even one were removed, I could not believe the structure would stand.

During that time I had my first serious doubts about Tami's motives. Why *had* she come here? Were we any closer to solving anything, or were we only headed toward the ending Dream Walker had warned me about?

I decided to wait a while longer and see what happened. Tami would be leaving soon and things might return to normal.

When Tami returned several hours later, she said she'd seen a huge blue bird fly in an "S" pattern over the river, then disappear. For some reason I doubted her.

I had no opportunity to speak about the things that were eating at me because the other two girls had arrived home from school., I wondered if Tami had planned it that way.

Greg arrived just before dinner. He and Tami went for a walk. Shortly thereafter, I heard them calling from across the road. They said strange melodic sounds were coming from the trees. I went to where they were standing. At first it sounded like an owl hooting, then dribbled off into the same long string of notes I'd heard from my bedroom several times during the night.

It sounded like a cross between a woman and a bird. We saw no sign of what was making the sounds.

Greg left early that night. He had a long drive to get home. Tami told me they were going to move in together. I was shocked. That meant she would have to quit her job in California and find one up here. She had known Greg for less than a week.

I was doing the dishes when I remembered there were some dirty cups in the living room. When I turned the corner, my stomach knotted at what I saw. John was lying on the floor with Tami astride him, rubbing his bare back. They were whispering like lovers. They both looked guilty when they realized I was there.

"This isn't what you think, Sal. Poor John is so sore. He's been chopping too much wood since your parents were here. Did I tell you I'm a licensed masseuse?"

John just smiled like he'd eaten the canary.

I didn't say a word, just picked up the cups and returned to the kitchen. I heard them whispering and giggling as I left. John told Tami that if it didn't work out with Greg he could fix up Youdi's cabin for her. I almost threw up in the sink. I felt like Tami was stealing my husband. She didn't want him; she had Greg. And John was eating it up.

I made no mention of what I'd seen when John came to bed. He went right to sleep. I didn't sleep at all that night.

In the morning, John left for work without speaking to me. Tami acted like nothing had happened. Youdi and Emily arrived about an hour later. I was so glad to see them I almost cried. We all talked at the kitchen table a while. It seemed like old times, except I could feel Youdi watching Tami.

Then Youdi said she needed to walk in the woods. She took off by herself, but came back only a short time later excited because she'd seen a heron flying in an "S" shaped pattern just before it disappeared. They both had said they saw the same thing. I didn't know what to think. Was I misjudging Tami again?

I brought out my heron feather and Tami did a reading from it: *"Birds... scouts... scanning the area. Star shaped formation. Toby standing within the star... light radiating... a tube of light streaming down on him... receiving the light. Some sort of transference. The birds are scouts, messengers sent from another dimension. At the same time, or no more than a few hours apart, a sighting will occur here in Washington. Toby will be responsible for a channeling of forces. Someone other than this group will be involved. A new person. That same person will give Youdi a circular object. December, new or full moon. Something major will happen. Around winter solstice."*

Greg came again that evening. I felt sorry for him and guilty because I had introduced him to Tami. At the same time, they seemed so smitten with each other. I had such conflicting feelings about Tami it was making me feel crazy. I hadn't had a chance to talk to Youdi about any of it. Tami was always there.

Greg spent the night on the couch so he could wake up early to drive Tami to the airport in Seattle the next morning. I heard them kissing and talking late into the night. What kind of life would Greg have if Tami hit on every man she came near? I was worried for Greg, and myself.

Early the next morning we walked to Greg's truck to say goodbye. When Tami hugged me, I could feel her touch a part of me where she did not have my permission to go. I wasn't sure I liked her touch anymore. “Thanks so much for everything.” Her smile was cunning, as if we shared a secret. “I have a feeling I’ll be back sooner than you think.”

She hugged John a little too long. Greg seemed not to notice. He was besotted. I breathed a sigh of relief as the truck disappeared down the road.

It was short-lived.

Tami called the next day to say that the oddest thing had happened. When she arrived home there was a letter waiting for her transferring her to the company’s Seattle office. She hadn’t requested a transfer yet. They had even given her a raise. Her laugh was chilling, “Isn’t it funny how things work out? You’ll be seeing a lot more of me in the future.”

My heart sank. I couldn’t have Tami living next door in Youdi’s cabin, even for a short time. The thought made me ill. In the time Tami had been here, it felt like she had taken over every aspect of my life. An old adage came to mind, “Be careful what you wish for.”

I felt threatened by the thought it would be permanent. How could Tami have gotten a job up here when she hadn’t even asked? The blood rushed to my face, then drained away, leaving a cold chill behind. Something was seriously wrong.

I decided to call Youdi. If I could make her understand what I was afraid of, maybe she could help me think of a solution. I knew she was my friend; Tami I wasn’t so sure of.

Youdi’s phone rang and rang. No one answered. I had the feeling dark forces, over which I had no control, were gathering like hungry wolves at the edge of the campfire.

For several days I tried to call Youdi. No one answered. Each night I awoke covered in sweat, after having a horrible dream. I couldn't recall what I had dreamed, but I knew it was the same each time. The last time this happened there was a burnt smell in the air. This was followed by a sizzling sound like a bug zapper. The smell clung to my nostrils as I waited in the darkness for my heart to slow.

In the morning I happened to glance at the dream catcher Youdi had given me. My stomach lurched when I saw that a hole was burned through the middle. I yanked it down and threw it in the woodstove, then raced to the phone to dial Youdi's number.

She answered as if she'd been waiting.

My fears came pouring out in a torrent of words. Youdi didn't speak until I was done. "Tami wants what you have. She will do anything to get it."

I didn't understand. "You mean John and the kids?"

"No. I'm speaking of who you are. You bring warmth and sunshine when you enter a room. I can see it around you like a nimbus. I saw it the day we met. I've watched, and others see it, too. When Tami enters a room, people stop talking. She brings with her the chill of a winter day. Haven't you noticed?"

"I thought it was because she's so pretty."

"No, my friend. It is because with her comes *masachie*... evil. People are chilled in her presence. It is something she cannot change. I saw it transfer from her to you the first day she touched you. She will take all the warmth from you if you are not careful. She tried to do the same to me when I was holding her hand during the reading the day I ran out. Like sucking the breath from a baby. I will talk to Paul and Toby to see what can be done about Tami. They have known her for a while: they may have insights we do not have."

I told Youdi what I had overheard John saying about Tami living in her cabin. "That will not happen. We will find *another* place for her to go if she does not go to live with Greg. Be careful until you hear from me again."

After I hung up, I thought long about what Youdi had said. Her words made sense. But when I talked to Tami, Tami's words made sense. Really, I was totally confused and nothing made sense. Was Youdi jealous of Tami? Was Tami jealous of Youdi? Both of them were acting strange. They were great teachers and I was learning so much from each of them. I wanted to believe them both, but that didn't work either.

Rather than wait for Youdi's help, I decided to do what I could to find Tami somewhere else to stay. In the local paper I found a small cabin for rent at the beginning of our road about two or three miles away. I called Tami to tell her. She seemed excited. "That's great. You're a good friend. I'll call right away. Even if Greg and I live at his house, we can always spend weekends there."

I didn't tell Tami I had spoken to Youdi about her, or that Youdi planned to speak to Paul and Toby. When I was talking to Tami, it was hard to believe the things Youdi had said. Maybe Tami was just a flirt. She hadn't actually done anything else. I liked her otherwise, and she seemed grateful I was her friend.

Tami's next statement knocked the air out of me. "There's something I need to tell you. One of the reasons I need to move is Paul. He won't leave me alone. I've told him I don't want to be involved with a married man, but he won't listen. I didn't say anything when I was up there because I know how you all respect him, especially Youdi. If I didn't feel so close to you, I wouldn't say anything, but I know I can trust you."

Tami was right. We had gotten close. What had I been thinking? She wasn't after John; she had Greg. What Tami said about Paul seemed odd to me, though. Paul and his wife had seemed so close. But I didn't really know them. Dear God... how would I tell Youdi?

Tami's next words made me think she could read my mind. "I wouldn't say anything to Youdi. She probably wouldn't believe you. Once I'm up there I won't have to deal with Paul's advances any longer. Until then this can be our little secret. If Youdi knew she would only spoil things for everyone."

Not tell Youdi? I guessed that was probably wise. But I'd never kept anything from Youdi, except for my journeys with Dream Walker. My mind was bouncing like a ping-pong ball. I didn't know what to do, or what to think. Things were a lot simpler before Youdi brought Tami here. After I hung up, I walked in circles, wrestling with my conflicting thoughts. I felt I was sitting on a time bomb. I didn't sleep much that night.

Youdi called back the next morning. She said she had talked to Paul. Under pressure he admitted that he had been having personal problems with Tami. Although she was a great researcher, she couldn't keep her hands to herself. He had told her he was happily married but she wouldn't leave him alone. He had confided to Youdi he would be glad when she moved. I didn't know what to say.

Youdi said she would try to work with Tami, but she could no longer trust her. She claimed she could put her personal feelings aside for the good of the group. Did this mean she was backing down on what she said about Tami trying to steal my warmth? I decided to put it all aside, too, and let things take their own course. I felt guilty about not being honest with Youdi, but I just wasn't sure what the problems were and I certainly didn't know how to solve them.

Youdi came out the next day with her son, Mic. He was making some repairs on her camp trailer up river at her other property. She said when they unlocked the door, it smelled burnt inside. On the cabinets, she found the same burn marks we had seen on the tree and Curt's body.

We took a walk to the river and discovered some odd markings in the sand. First there was a capital H about four inches high. On a rock nearby were several symbols: a capital A with no centerline, a dot, then a capital I, a long sideways capital S and another dot. A little farther on was a circle the size of a pie with an exclamation point and another vertical line inside. There were no footprints near except those of a dog and some deer, so we wondered how the symbols had gotten there.

It was too cold and windy for sane people to be out walking on the beach, but Youdi and I trudged along, hunkered into our coats. I found myself watching the woods out of the corner of my eye, as if by doing so I would see something I would have otherwise missed. The voice of the wind was almost articulate, but I couldn't quite catch the words. The great, gray boulders along the water's edge watched me knowingly as I clambered over their smooth surfaces. The only sound was the moaning of the tall trees as a gust of wind rippled along the ridge. I could smell change in the air.

Youdi and I walked in silence, becoming one with our surroundings and each other. On our way back, the woods shimmered like a mirage in the encroaching fog. The wind died down and lights were visible in the distance. As we walked toward our cabins, the gates of mist parted for us to pass, then closed silently behind us. Just before we reached home, a high-pitched scream echoed through the gray depths behind.

I began to feel uneasy. I glanced at Youdi and we quickened our steps. A pungent smell rode in on the fog. Fir sap, moss, and ancient earth were overpowered by the intense animal smell we knew well.

Skookum was near.

Chapter Twenty

The snows that are older than history,
The woods where the weird shadows slant;
The stillness, the moonlight, the mystery,
I've bade 'em goodbye — but I can't.

— Robert W. Service
"The Spell of the Yukon"

Youdi, Emily, and Mic's girlfriend Natalie came out on November 8th for my birthday. It was a beautiful morning, hazy with a hard frost. It was too cold for any of us to venture out, except Youdi. She went for a walk while the rest of us sat and talked in my living room. I nursed the reluctant fire to life.

The wind came up after Youdi had been gone a couple of hours. We began to be anxious for her safety when she burst through the door. "Do you still have your plaster of Paris? I found a huge three-toed print across the road."

I hopped up to get it, but I could tell when I picked up the box it was useless. Water had seeped into the box and all I had now was a big, white doorstop.

"It's okay," Youdi said. "I'll have Curt pick some up tomorrow. He and Emily can bring it out."

This seemed odd. Perhaps distance had mellowed Curt's fears about returning. "I do have some film in the camera," I said. "At least we can get photos."

I ran to find the camera and a ruler. We all bundled up and Youdi retraced the route she had taken earlier. We walked around the corner of the tiny, demolished shack across the road on the side of the path so as not to disturb anything. The trail ran parallel to the road after that and we ended up across the road from Emily's old house.

The day before, two of John's friends from work had come out to look at the truck he was selling. While they waited for him to come out, they claimed they had heard whistles and low, moaning noises coming from the woods across the road. They said they'd heard the same sounds on a TV show about Bigfoot recently. They left without ever looking at John's truck, making excuses and driving off fast.

I told the others about this as we walked. The wind had picked up even more since we left the cabin. It sliced through our layers of clothing like icy needles. By the time we reached a series of deep scuffmarks where the grass had been torn away, we were cold to the bone.

Youdi pointed to the three-toed print. I placed the ruler beside it and had her place her foot so it would be included in the photo. I clicked off three pictures in rapid succession, then we ran for the cabin as hail beat down on our heads.

Curt and Emily came out the next day with fresh plaster of Paris, but it had rained all night. The original print was unrecognizable, but they took casts of two new ones they'd found on the same trail. The casts came out looking like a kindergarten project. I hoped the photos were better.

The rains came again with a vengeance. As I sat looking out at the dripping, fog-covered forest, I realized Tami would be back soon. I wasn't sure if I was glad or not. Life had been simpler before Tami.

She and Greg called often. They seemed excited about their future together. Tami had rented the cabin down the road and I had been sent a key so I could see that everything was in order before her arrival.

She and Greg planned to use it on weekends once she moved in with him in Gig Harbor. That way she could still be close to the action.

Youdi called one evening just before Thanksgiving to see if I'd go with her to a monthly meeting held by a man named Ed Kellogg, who lived in Seattle. Ed wrote a Bigfoot newsletter and had a museum filled with Bigfoot artifacts. I had to decline Youdi's invitation because Amber was ill, but I asked for a rain check for the next month.

Paul called later the same evening to talk about a new researcher they had recruited. His name was Jack. In the past, Jack had worked with some Bigfoot researchers in The Dalles, Oregon. Now he worked for the Forest Service. It seemed he was quite knowledgeable in the fields of plants and wildlife. He would be in our area soon and would be out to investigate and talk to all of us. Paul never mentioned Tami. Neither did I.

There were secrets in our group. I didn't like the fact, but until it interfered with our research, I didn't really care who was to blame for what.

Snow fell on Thanksgiving. It was warm and cozy in our cabin, with the smell of roasting turkey and my family around. I hadn't felt so contented since before Tami came.

I took a short walk through the silent flakes before dinner. Breathing deep, I filled my nostrils with the sharp, clear air of the forest. This weather was a far cry from the flood-ravaged days of the year before. Across the valley, I could make out the big root wad where John and Pete had seen Skookum. Then I remembered that Amber had seen one there, too. A lot had happened since that day. I thought of something Dream Walker had said to me on our first journey, "I will help you remember how to walk as one with the forest. This will be my gift to you." He had certainly done that and so much more. I could use his wisdom now.

I still searched the mirror for a sign of his wrinkled face. I guessed I always would. My hand went to the necklace at my throat as I headed home to give thanks with my family.

The days seemed to fly by. Youdi came out a couple of times and we went for long walks together. It was like old times. Nothing had occurred in the last few weeks, but we searched all the same.

One morning, as we crunched through the snow to the water's edge, I noticed that the whole valley was like a fairyland of crystal. Overnight the temperature had dipped into the teens. Then a wind had come up after fog had settled to ground level in the canyon. The result was a hoar frost, freezing the fog to the naked stems of the bushes and laden boughs of the evergreens and turning the landscape into a wonderland of twinkling ice. Until now, I had only heard of this phenomenon.

I looked out over the river, then blinked and looked again. In one certain spot, the air shimmered, as it does when there is intense heat. There was certainly no heat out here. It was as though I was seeing through a distorted window to a world beyond. I had heard of spots like this: a warp between two dimensions, a place where things can come through from one world to another. I shook Youdi by the shoulder, “Look. Do you see what I see?”

“Aiyee... the old ones spoke of such places. They were called *ooahut yahwa* – the trail to beyond. Both good and evil could use such a trail. It was said Skookum used such portals to disappear when danger threatened. This is a *hyas tamanous* place... highly magical. We should feel honored to have seen it.”

Fingers of fog caressed the trees as we made our way home. That night my nightmares began again. Icicles tinkled like wind chimes at the corners of the cabin and the wind howled at the windows. I snuggled deeper into the warm covers, but I could not escape the dreams when they came.

I found myself standing behind Youdi's cabin, wrapped in a blanket. It covered me like a shroud. A shape moved through the moon shadows, its ears tuned to the whispers of the night. Off in the distance a dog howled. Then, as suddenly as it had begun, it stopped. Silence lay upon the night.

Thin clouds drifted across the moon. When they had moved on, I realized I was not the only one watching. Tami stood only a few feet away, her eyes riveted on the slowly moving shape ahead on the path.

Tami had not seen my approach.

A cloud shifted, and I could see that the shape ahead was Youdi. She was naked and freezing. She appeared to be lost, her expression desperate. I wanted to go to her, wrap her in my blanket, and hold her close until she stopped her violent shaking, but I found I couldn't move.

The wind rose, pushing tendrils of hair across Tami's face with frigid fingers. I had the queer feeling that Tami commanded the wind, coaxing it to rise and blow harder as she watched Youdi freezing on the path.

Tami sensed my presence then. She spoke without ever turning her head. "Oh, hello there. Looks like we're in for a storm. Better bundle up." Then she turned to look at me. She had a look of pure glee and a catlike smile on her face. The cold I felt was not from the wind.

I woke up sweating.

Greg called the next night to say he was picking Tami up at the airport the following afternoon. The emotional aftereffects of my dream still clung to the edges of my mind. I hoped it was only a dream, but it had felt so real I wasn't looking forward to seeing Tami.

I thought I'd feel better if I called Youdi and heard that she was all right. I wouldn't mention the dream.

Youdi sounded awful when she answered. "Oh Sal, I'm glad you called. I won't be able to come out there tomorrow after all. I must have caught an awful chill last night. I'm running a high fever. Say hello to everyone for me."

My stomach turned. I could hardly speak. "I'm so sorry. I'll call back tomorrow to see how you are. Take care of yourself."

I felt sick at heart. Ever since I'd known Youdi she had never been sick. I thought again of my dream. Could Tami have done this somehow? She was fifteen hundred miles away. Did she dislike Youdi that much? Did she really have that kind of power?

That night the dreams came again.

At first, Youdi and I were walking by the river. Then I was alone in a part of the forest I was unfamiliar with. Fog drifted in, circling my feet, climbing up my legs like ropes. I found I couldn't move. The harder I struggled, the tighter I was held. The fog engulfed me, dragging me into its clammy depths. I couldn't catch my breath.

I was prone and gasping when the fog lifted. When my breathing had returned to normal, I noticed a faint green light glowing off to my right. Believing it to be a yard light from a nearby house, I headed slowly in that direction. I knew if I could recognize a house, I could find my way home.

The light wavered bright and dim as the mist swirled in front of me, but I kept it in sight. When I tripped over a boulder, I realized I'd been going in the wrong direction. I had come to the river. "But there aren't any lights at the river," I said to myself. "The Duncan's house was washed away in the flood."

I crawled cautiously over the rocks, guided only by the green glow ahead until I reached the water. The light was coming from the other side. I searched the fog, trying to determine the source. The mist parted, and there stood "Biggy." My heart thumped as we looked at each other.

His face reflected wisdom and dignity. It looked human. Much more human than the men who sought to kill him so they could prove he existed.

The Skookum raised his hand in farewell, then turned towards the trees. Shots rang out. I watched in horror as he fell to the ground then vanished. The glow faded and mist covered the spot where he had stood. It was the shimmering spot where Youdi and I had seen the trail to beyond.

I was alone in the night, but now I had my bearings. When I reached our cabin, Dream Walker was standing by the steps to the deck. His thoughts came to me, "Skookum have left this valley to find a place of safety. They will return when the one with sunbeams in her hair comes to search for them. When that day comes I will be here to guide her."

I awoke to find my pillow drenched in tears.

That afternoon when Tami and Greg arrived I found myself glad to see her. Somehow I had convinced myself that Youdi's illness and my nightmare had no connection. I missed the journeys of the mind that Tami and I took together. That was the kind of power she had over me.

John seemed only mildly interested in the fact that Tami had returned. He seemed happier to see Greg. The two of them sat in the living room having a beer while I took Tami to see her cabin. Together we carried in her few belongings. The rest would arrive by truck the next day. Her phone was already hooked up.

“I’m so glad to be back.” Tami said. “I just know I’m going to love living here. You’ve done such a nice job making the house ready for me. Have you heard from Paul lately?”

That’s a strange question. I thought.

“Uh, no. I haven’t talked to him for a while. He calls Youdi now and then. He and Toby have a new researcher working with them. Someone named Jack. He’ll be up here to talk to all of us soon.”

Tami seemed like she wasn’t really listening. “Um, that’s nice. And how is Youdi feeling?”

My heart skipped a beat. “Not very well. That’s why she couldn’t come today.”

“That’s a shame. I thought Indians had better sense than to go out in the cold without warm clothing. Well, we’d better go see what the boys are doing.”

I followed her dumbly out the door. How could Tami have possibly known how Youdi got sick? Unless...

When we got home, Tami all but devoured Greg with kisses. John stood up and left the room. I stayed, but felt uncomfortable. They soon left to spend the night at Tami’s cabin. I felt relieved when they were gone.

I called Youdi and Emily told me she was too ill to talk.

Over the next couple of weeks, I spoke to Youdi a few times, as she fought her way back to health. Tami was busy with Greg.

Christmas was only a few days away when Youdi called one evening to ask if I still planned to go with her to the monthly meeting at Ed Kellogg's. I was happy she was well enough to go. I said I'd love to.

The same evening Tami knocked on my door. She seemed upset. "Greg and I are no longer seeing each other," was all she said. I was curious to know what had happened, but something in her attitude told me not to ask. Tami changed the subject by asking if I knew my way around Seattle. She said she was planning to rent an apartment there.

"No, I don't know where anything is, but Youdi and I are going to Seattle tomorrow to attend a meeting." I was instantly sorry. Tami's face brightened.

"Do you think Youdi would mind if I came along?" She asked. "I might meet someone who knows of a place for rent."

I was surprised by Tami's complete mood change. "Uh... I don't know. I'll have to call Youdi to see."

Youdi hesitated when I told her why I had called, but she agreed Tami could come along.

When John came home from work the next day, Tami and I drove to Tacoma to pick Youdi up. I didn't receive my usual hug and Youdi was silent on the way to Seattle. So was Tami. I tried to fill the void by chattering nervously. It was difficult to think of anything to say. Youdi gave directions as I wound my way through the unfamiliar streets of the big city. I was relieved when we arrived, for many reasons.

It proved to be an interesting evening. People from several states told of their Bigfoot experiences. One of the speakers was a researcher named René Dahinden. He had been in the field for many years. He knew Paul well. They didn't agree on much, but then not many researchers did. One thing they all had in common was their opinion of James.

We had been at the meeting only a few minutes when a tall, good-looking man came over and introduced himself as Jack. He talked to Youdi, Tami, and me for a few minutes, then went off to talk with some of the other people in the room. When I looked for Tami later, she and Jack were huddled in a corner of the couch talking. They remained together for the rest of the evening.

The meeting began to break up about ten o'clock. Tami came toward us, her expression glowing, "You girls go ahead and leave whenever you want. Jack said he would drive me home later."

"That was fast," Youdi muttered.

"She must be lonely. I don't know what happened between Tami and Greg, but you can't blame her for trying to find someone else."

Youdi gave me funny look and shook her head, "You just don't get it, do you Sal?"

We drove home in silence.

I didn't see Tami much after that night. She moved to Seattle. She and Jack spent weekends at the cabin down the road, but they never came by.

John made several attempts to contact Greg, but no one ever answered. We never heard from Greg again.

I wasn't surprised to find my life had much less turmoil with Tami absent. John seemed to return to himself once he realized

Tami had never been interested in him. I think he felt like a fool. Soon it was almost like we had never met Tami. Except for Youdi.

Youdi never came to the river or called me anymore. One day I phoned her. Her once cheery voice sounded strained and distant. It was like talking to a stranger. I asked when she was coming out.

Her answer was short, and to the point. “Not for awhile. I’m busy. I’ll be in touch.”

I felt hollow after I hung up; like someone had died. When I went out to get an armload of wood, I looked over at Youdi’s cabin. It sat lifeless, like I felt.

Several weeks went by with no word from Youdi. The first fragile haze of green burst forth on the trees. Violets and bleeding hearts filled the nooks and crannies of the forest once again. This was the time I’d been waiting for. Skookum would return to the river on their yearly migration. I knew Youdi would soon follow. Like me, she couldn’t stay away.

Each time a car drove down the road I ran to the window. Each time I walked to the river I expected to see Youdi sitting on a boulder, waiting for me to join her. I held my breath when I smelled wood smoke, hoping it came from Youdi’s campfire. The days dragged by, but Youdi never came.

Hers wasn’t the only absence I felt that spring. No screams split the still, crisp air at night. No chirping birds interrupted my slumber. No heavy footsteps shook the waterbed. The forest was quiet, but it wasn’t waiting. It was empty. It was just a forest.

The dogwoods were in bloom when Youdi’s letter came. I opened it slowly, as if I knew what it contained.

My dear friend,

I cannot risk coming to the river, so I must say goodbye in a letter. Your friend Tami is not what you think her to be. She has called upon forces beyond her control. Remember your mother's experience in my cabin? Tami will cause you great harm if you do not distance yourself from her.

I have reason to fear her abilities. If I choose to ignore these warnings, I stand to lose all that I hold dear. I won't come to see you again. I will always treasure the time we spent together. Tell no one I have contacted you. Burn my letter after you have read it, and scatter the ashes away from your cabin.

Youdi

Somehow, this letter put everything into place. Tami had succeeded in her quest to steal my joy. I slumped to the floor, sobbing. Once again, I felt like a ghost in another time, only this time I was alone.

I hadn't even seen Tami in weeks. How could Youdi desert me... leaving me to fight the enemy alone? I knew the answer. I had seen the answer in my dream. Tami was dangerous in ways beyond my understanding.

I was engulfed by a wave of revulsion. I had been blinded by my thirst for knowledge and the flattery and attention of someone who had claimed to be a friend and teacher. How could I have ignored one of the foremost rules of psychic awareness: trust your gut feelings?

All the warnings washed over me then, stark and obvious. Youdi's reluctance to have anything to do with Tami after that first day... the night of terror my mother had spent in Youdi's cabin fighting a sort of psychic warfare... Tami's maneuvering to drive a wedge between John and me...

I had opened the very core of my being to a monster. It had never occurred to me that the very abilities I sought to harness would be used with selfish intent to harm the ones I loved.

Even Dream Walker had warned me, How could I have not seen what was so obvious to others? I felt like a fool.

As a gesture of friendship to Youdi, I burned her letter as she had asked and scattered the ashes in the river. I watched as they swirled away into the distance. Then I felt Tami enter my mind. She didn't ask permission, she just opened the door and walked in. That's when I made my decision.

When I got home, I went directly to my herb cabinet and grabbed up some bundles of sage. I walked to the road and lit one, then blew out the flame. My heart lifted as I smelled the sacred smoke.

With the bundle of sage continuing to give off smoke, I walked the boundaries of both Youdi's property and ours. It might be too little, too late, but I hoped the protective, cleansing powers of the smoke would help in the days to come.

When I finished, I wasn't sure if it had been enough, but I felt better. At least there was some hope.

That afternoon the phone rang. I knew who it would be. Tami's sugary voice came over the line, "It's me, Sal. I had the feeling you were ill. I know we haven't spent very much time together lately, but all that will change soon. Jack and I have been busy settling in. We'll be by to see you soon."

I summoned my courage. "It might be better if you waited a while, Tami. There's nothing going on in the area anyway. John was offered a job out of state, so we'll be moving soon," I lied. I didn't care if Tami believed me or not. There was silence on the line.

"Well, maybe I'll come to say goodbye before you leave."

The line went dead. I didn't care. I was afraid, but what could Tami do to me that would be worse that what she had already done?

The next few months were a blur. I didn't hear from Youdi or Tami. During the summer the people who owned the cabin on the other side of us came out to stay for several weeks. I had never even seen them before. They brought the worst of the city with them. Motorcycles buzzed like angry bees up and down the road. Shots rang out in staccato bursts from automatic weapons. Dogs and screaming children swarmed across our property chasing our ducks and chickens.

John came home one day and suggested we sell out and move. I didn't argue. Over the last few months, I had been no more than a robot, going through the motions of life. Everything I had here was shattered. I told John to call a realtor. We listed our cabin the same day.

The next weekend I saw Paul's rig on the road. Youdi's car followed. My heart flared to life, until I watched them drive on by.

We received several offers on our property within the first week. John and I rented a car, hired a sitter, and began the search for another house. When we topped the rise of a hill by the Umpqua River in Oregon, I knew we had found our new home. The rundown farmhouse was meant to be ours.

The cabin sold to an elderly couple a few days later.

I was packing when I heard a familiar knock at the door. "I could not let you leave without saying goodbye," Youdi said. Beside her stood Emily.

I wanted to ask Youdi why she had brought Tami here in the first place. I wanted to ask why we couldn't start over and still be friends, but my throat felt gripped by an invisible hand and the words wouldn't come.

Faced with only my silence, they turned and left. I dropped to the floor and cried until I thought I would die.

On the day we were to leave, I walked to the river one last time. It was early morning, and the mist had not yet lifted. It twined around my ankles as if trying to hold me there. I stood drinking in the valley as I heard Dream Walker's parting words in my mind once more. "If anyone can make a difference, it is you, Sallal."

"Well, I certainly made a mess of this one, old friend," I said out loud. I turned and walked home.

The next day we left the Valley of the Skookum.

Epilogue

May you always unfold your night wings wide
And treasure the visions of the Dreamer.

— Mary Summer Rain
"Spirit Song"

It has been twenty-five years since we left the valley, yet sometimes the smallest thing can send me hurtling back in time to those days. I can taste the mornings, smell the wood smoke, and see the misty pathways in my mind's eye. There will never be another place such as that for me. Magic happens only once in a person's lifetime... if they are lucky.

My daughter was ten years old when she first discovered a box in the back of my closet. It contained all I had left of those magical days but my memories. Over the years, she would bring out the box and ask me to tell her all that I could remember. At first, I was reluctant, because it still hurt too much, but slowly the story unfolded.

One day I looked at the young woman sitting next to me and I saw the sun shining from *within* her yellow hair. I knew then that both she and I had heard the same echo in time. I realized my story was a living, breathing thing with roots in the past and branches that spread into the future. I saw my daughter's destiny as I remembered Dream Walker's words, "To one of you has been born a girl child with sunbeams in her hair. I will come to her one day and she will learn the ways of Skookum. Much time will pass and this child will take many false paths before she wears the pendant of Sallal. But one day she will walk in the footsteps of Skookum and gaze on the autumn star."

It was time for the mysteries to begin again. I reached into my dresser drawer and pulled out a small velvet box. I opened it and handed the pendant to my daughter, Autumn Star. Then I summoned up my courage and went to call Youdi.

An Invitation

The history you have just read describes events experienced by my family and friends during the late 1970s. The locations are real as well. The names of some characters have been changed for privacy and other reasons. I wrote this story so my youngest daughter could know of those times. I don't know if all of the various events I've written about are related to Bigfoot, but they happened in the same place during the same time, in the Valley of the Skookum.

I know I came away with more questions than answers.

As a result of her childhood experiences, my youngest daughter, Autumn Williams, has had a burning interest in the Bigfoot phenomenon. For the past sixteen years she has gathered reports and evidence and interviewed countless eyewitnesses, many of whom, like our own family have experienced much more than a brief glimpse of a creature on a dark road. Autumn is now one of the foremost Bigfoot researchers in the country.

If you would like to report a sighting, you can contact Autumn at her website: www.OregonBigfoot.com. If you have questions or comments about my story, you can contact me through my publisher: Idyll Arbor, PO Box 720, Ravensdale, WA 98051.